To Jeffery Stinson (1933–2008)
and Christian Klemt (1955–2006)

place and occasion
Montgomery Sisam Architects

To Terry,
With gratitude for keeping us
medically sound (or almost) in the
formative years.
Hope you and Davia are well and
that you will enjoy this monograph.
Best,
David + Terry

Artifice
books on architecture

contents

introduction

Whatever space and time mean, place and occasion mean more. For space in the image of man is place and time in the image of man is occasion. Aldo van Eyck

The process of preparing this book has been very rewarding. It has caused us to take the time to step back and examine an entire body of work; to probe the content, find the patterns and clarify the themes. These the reader will find in the body of the book. There are, however, three lenses that will provide context for why we do what we do.

The first lens is the social and cultural context that shaped our beginning. Toronto and Canada in the 1960s and 70s were places of great hope and optimism. Expo '67 exposed the country to some of the best and most exciting architecture in the world at the time. The opening of the skies to inexpensive commercial travel brought architects from the UK and Europe to teach us and allowed us to tour as students in return. The ground-breaking educator Peter Prangnell—fresh in from England by way of Harvard and Columbia Universities—had a profound impact at the University of Toronto, while Prime Minister Pierre Trudeau inspired the entire country to dream of a socially "Just Society". As architects this led us to dream that buildings—and their collective gathering into public space—could participate in the health and well-being of individuals and society as a whole. We became interested in making architecture that emerged from an understanding of human behaviour, not only in the functional sense, but in the socio/political and poetic sense as well; an architecture both of and for human beings.

For our practice this means the design process begins with a thorough investigation of the following: how will the building be used, experienced and make one feel, where it will be located, what are the social and political forces shaping it and who will pay for it? A dialogue that includes all who have any influence over the project or who will be affected by it, no matter their position or role, is essential to shape and define the meaning of a building. We know that architecture is more able to support the transformation of social good when it emerges from this inclusive, often dialectic process, first and foremost.

The second lens is our commitment to running a democratic studio; a democracy of shared values, free of the cult of the individual and free of architectural creeds or dogma. We govern ourselves using common sense and the best available evidence. We encourage everyone in the practice to think for themselves and use their voice.

We acknowledge that each building is the result of 1,000 decisions, with each decision requiring creative and critical thinking. We recognise that the more minds included in the process the better the yield of good ideas. This is distinct from 'design by committee' by virtue of treating the studio as a teaching ground where everyone is both student and teacher. In other words, our culture of mutual respect means decisions are made based on merit, not vote. Since our inception we have also grown and now have people of all ages from 12 different countries, reflective of the multicultural fabric of Canada and of Toronto in particular.

The third lens is our ambition to do more with less. We work and rework the design; always striving to simplify and clarify that which is essential to meet the stated goals and aspirations. We have found that the simplest solution is often the most cost effective, a process that thrives in the not-for-profit environments in which we primarily work.

At the end we see our role as architects as a noble pursuit; one that is embedded in the social fabric. A pursuit requiring skill and experience to nudge and prod something that was once nothing into something of value; to make an empty space into a meaningful place. To paraphrase TS Eliot, there are and always will be "a hundred visions and revisions/before the taking of the toast and tea".

architecture as citizen
beth kapusta

When I am asked the question critics are so often posed about favourite Toronto buildings, I have surprised myself, for the last few years, by launching into a passionate appreciation of a building that many find an unusual choice. It could not be considered in any way a signature building, exuberant formal expression, notable landmark, paragon of material or technical inventiveness, or architectural novelty.

Yet it remains firmly atop my list for a simple human reason: as a building, it is a good citizen. It sits well on its site, it reaches out to its community through programming and sensible massing. It opens itself to the abundant nature its site avails; it is redolent with a sense of warmth, community, natural light. It integrates art into everyday life. Its design is the culmination of deep, experiential insights and telegraphs a harmonious idealism that cannot happen without a strong client relationship.

The building is Holland Bloorview Kids Rehabilitation Hospital, and the agent largely responsible for these very human factors is Montgomery Sisam Architects.[1]

A Short History:
Long Term Care, and a Broadening Spectrum

A closer look at the subtle legacy of Montgomery Sisam Architects sees many of these essential human themes woven through the philosophical fibre of the firm's work. Founded in 1978 as Stinson Montgomery Sisam, the practice established itself doing work in library and public building additions and renovations and in long term care, providing design leadership characterised by the humanisation of care facilities.

An adaptive reuse project for Facelle Company Ltd's Head Offices was the firm's first substantial project, foreshadowing many recurrent architectural themes—an open, egalitarian plan inspired by the idea of a village, the location of public circulation on the building perimeter, the economical introduction of light through simple light monitors.

After Jeff Stinson left the partnership in 1987 to form a new practice and focus on teaching at the University of Toronto, where all three had taught architecture, the firm continued to thrive and grow under the leadership of Terry Montgomery and David Sisam, imbued with the idealism of the 1960s, and underpinned by design principles the founding principals saw emerging in British, Dutch and Scandinavian architecture.

The practice subsequently maintained a consistent backbone of long term and healthcare design work that has ebbed and flowed with demographic trends and political will. The Ontario government's commitment to long term care facilities propelled the firm's growth from a constant of about 12 or 13 employees through the first decade, to over 40, where it remains. Ownership of the firm expanded to seven principals between 2000 and 2007.[2]

With a reputation for team collaboration and client service, Montgomery Sisam's later work would cover a much more eclectic spectrum of building types: bridges, a yacht

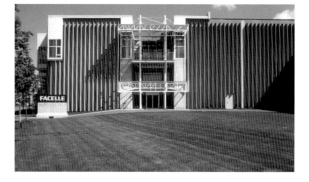

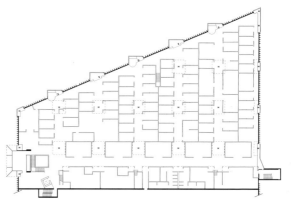

OPPOSITE TOP **Adaptive reuse of an industrial warehouse for the corporate headquarters for Facelle Company Ltd.**

OPPOSITE BOTTOM **Facelle Company Ltd plan. The plan is organised around a prime north–south corridor with support space and meeting rooms and public circulation with sitting bays on the perimeter. Offices borrow daylight from large roof monitors over the columns.**

TOP **Bird watchers gather at Bird Studies Canada Headquarters.**

BOTTOM **Bathurst Clark Library.**

1. Montgomery Sisam Architects in a joint venture with Stantec Architecture.

2. In 1999, Robert Davies and Ed Applebaum joined as principals, followed by Santiago Kunzle and Christian Klemt in 2001, Alice Liang in 2006 and Daniel Ling in 2007. Christian Klemt died in 2006.

3. Montgomery Sisam Architects in a joint venture with Farrow Partnership Architects.

club, a bird studies headquarters, libraries, botanical gardens, university buildings, park pavilions, as well as rehabilitation, complex continuing care and mental health facilities.

A typical Montgomery Sisam project (if there is such a thing, as the desire for 'signature' buildings is not something to which the principals aspire) generally lacks a lavish budget or extravagant materiality.

If pressed to find a common architectonic thread, I would instead point to assembly preferences like the consistent appearance of a solid, almost workman-like base, upon which the more expressive elevational features play (the elaboration of this foundational theme of anchoring is interesting to trace from an early project—Bathurst Clark Library—through Bob Rumball Home for the Deaf, St John's Rehab Hospital[3] and the Convent for the Sisterhood of St John the Divine.

More than being a compositional motif, there is always a sense of modest anchoring to this material gesture, a foil to the inevitable moment where underlying social idealism strongly expresses itself, where architecture becomes an act of community.

I think of the unlikely public space, for instance, at the Bird Studies Canada Headquarters at Long Point, a simple, sheltered outdoor room intersection at the convergence of the research building's two long wings, where birdwatchers and researchers come together overlooking a UNESCO biosphere reserve to observe, study and exchange stories of their latest sightings. I have a particular affinity for the knowing simplicity of this gesture, as someone who finds myself enjoying a picnic on this deck each year, during the annual migration that takes place as tundra swans migrate from southern climes to their summering grounds in the Arctic. Just as Long Point itself acts as a vital hinge in this journey, so too this sheltered place is a nexus of recreation and science, knowledge and community, skillfully buffered against the prevailing winds, yet open to the poetry of the adjacent wetland and distant Lake Erie.

Another good example of this is the main gathering space at the Greenwood College School, where a summer camp-like great hall is bracketed by a fireplace at one end and a climbing wall at the other, with a sensibility that manages to be rustic and urbane at the same time, and conveys a highly spirited and holistic idea of the spaces and relationships that are at the root of learning.

Or the convivial space framed by the suspension cables of the Humber River Bridge, a floating plaza that is another

beloved room in the city of Toronto (former mayor David Miller singled it out as his favourite spot in the city in his 2010 memoir *Witness to a City*). His words capture beautifully the public essence of this 'people's bridge' as an ideological entity:

It symbolises the idea that investment in public goods, and the public realm, permanently benefits all of us.... The Humber River Bridge stands for the idea that public investments in great public places have enduring value, and that public money can and should be invested in beautiful places that benefit us all.

Design Empathy and Experiential Research: Architectural Facets of Citizenship

There is an interesting phenomenon of design empathy that focuses the firm's work on subtle but important facets of human experience and interaction. I cannot help but think this aspect of Montgomery Sisam's work would have done Jane Jacobs proud: the application of relevant human experience augmenting professional expertise to increase the ability of design to enhance the human condition.

Take, for example, the experiential richness of a project like Belmont House, a long term care and seniors' residence in downtown Toronto, which is palpable 25 years after its design. Testament to the value of a longstanding relationship (subsequent changes and additions continue to be stewarded by the office), the building still impresses as a deeply human place, with generous natural light, and a strong sense of community established through outdoor courtyards and the primacy afforded interior common areas—and the small touches of humanity that relieve the institutional feeling typical of such places. Already emergent are Montgomery Sisam leitmotifs such as every corridor ending in light, and the emphasis on creating a residential rather than a clinical sensibility—themes that re-emerge in some of their later work in mental health.

The firm would go on to a more systematised application of these design principles in the dozens of long term care facilities they designed across the province and beyond, with clients that included regional and municipal homes, various charitable organisations and private providers such as Extendicare, with a studied approach to creating a more home-like sensibility that included a detailed review of material choices, colours, and the type of lighting and hardware fixtures.

They are not the kind of places so 'designed' that they feel incongruous with old-style comfy furniture, although the idiom leans towards a quiet modernism that tries to express structural moments where it makes sense, particularly in public areas. In a quietly wise way, these are the kind of places in which we can imagine our own parents looking comfortable, and even ourselves when the time comes.

Experiential research would take on an even more pronounced role in later projects. The design team of Holland Bloorview Kids Rehabilitation Hospital, for example, spent a whole day in wheelchairs as part of their research, so that the integration of everything from artwork (including on the ceiling, where it can be seen by patients on stretchers) to the design of nursing stations reflects, celebrates and elevates the reality that many of the users experience.

More recently, experiential research informed the design of Ronald McDonald House, a home for families with children undergoing medical treatment in Toronto. There is a deftness of touch in the way residential and personalising elements are injected into the design sensibility, whether it be the inclusion of sitting nooks on a surprisingly homey stairway, or the incorporation of chalk boards at the entry doors to each unit (there is also a version of this known as 'memory boxes' beside the long term care bedroom doors). Or the well-researched thoughtfulness of the common cooking areas, where directly observing the challenges of using the existing facilities led to a novel approach to make the cooking and eating areas high-functioning places of community that also engender enough sense of ownership that people look after them.

This tendency to actively engage in the issues that architecture touches extends to projects like the Centre for Addiction and Mental Health (CAMH) in Toronto, where the wholesale reform of facilities for mental health patients are also becoming less overtly institutional and more home-like.[4] This is done by integrating them into the community, and represents a middle ground between the polarising pendulum swings of over-institutionalisation and de-institutionalisation that characterised the previous architectural expressions of mental health facilities.

This project spans an 11-year period of consultation, design, research, and collaboration with a large design team. For two to three years, the design team did nothing but work with patients and clients, with the core team 'shadowing' the

staff, front-line nurses, engaging in activities like art therapy with clients, and bringing almost dollhouse-like, large-scale foam models from unit to unit as a tool of engagement, giving the team an extremely immersive introduction to mental health issues.

Understanding triggers of behavioural issues from an architectural perspective, particularly how the meanness of dimensions and lack of activities aggravated certain responses (pacing, agitation) was an important driver of design. The design team set about expanding personal choices for clients, designing configurations that would maximise options to gather with peers or be alone, thereby minimising boredom.

The first phase incorporates in-patient facilities on a module of six patients (after experimenting with groupings of 12, and eight, it was the closest cluster to a family unit that would also correspond to an optimal overall staffing number of 24). This decision has been further validated by post-occupancy evaluations, a follow-up research tool which is relatively rare in architectural practice.

Within the context of a larger mental health debate that strives to find a balance between human treatment of clients and the need for safety and security, humanising moments emerge, connecting people to the outdoors as a way of mitigating boredom. For instance, an intergenerational ground-level garden where children's out-patient programmes, geriatric mental health patients, and adolescent in-patients share space. Outdoor terraces are located on every floor so that staff members don't have to escort clients outdoors.

Practical, Incremental, Integrated:
Three Dimensions of Sustainability

Sustainability in all its political and physical dimensions looms large as another realm in which Montgomery Sisam's ideas of community, experiential education, contribution and voluntarism are inextricably wrapped together.

The office's architectural approach to sustainability is rooted in an intuitive, low-tech response first and foremost, with a palpable avoidance of more technical approaches. The mainstays of this integrated approach: narrow floor plates and operable windows, public circulation on the perimeter (to connect people psychologically to the outdoors, and reduce the need for artificial light and mechanical cooling). Deliberate simplicity, grounded in values and attitudes dating back to,

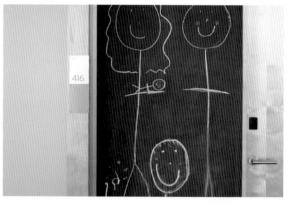

TOP **The 'lodge' at Greenwood College School.**

MIDDLE **Ronald McDonald House Toronto, chalkboard at room entry.**

BOTTOM **Centre for Addiction and Mental Health, aerial view of the competition-winning proposal.**

4. First phase: Montgomery Sisam Architects as part of the joint venture team C3 (Kuwabara Payne McKenna Blumberg Architects, Montgomery Sisam Architects and Kearns Mancini Architects). Second phase: C3+ Cannon Design—Planning, Design and Compliance Architects; Stantec Architecture Design, Build, Finance and Maintain Consortium Architects.

5. The firm was awarded the prestigious June Callwood Outstanding Achievement Award for Voluntarism in 2010 in recognition of this contribution.

and inspired by Steward Brand's *Whole Earth Catalogue*, underpins Montgomery Sisam's search for "economy of means and generosity of ends".

A good example is the Restoration Services Centre building in Vaughan, the firm's first LEED® Platinum building, interestingly achieved using largely low-tech means: limiting western exposure to reduce heat gain, maximising north light, controlling south light through a deep overhang as well as the familiar refrains of narrow floor plate and natural ventilation.

These simple things, along with composting toilets and a segregated septic loop for grey water, create an aggregate of factors that leads to a building that consumes far less energy, and dramatically minimises water usage. The project serves as a living example of the economic argument for sustainability: with an overall construction investment premium of less than ten per cent, the building uses 20 per cent of the natural gas, 70 per cent of the electricity, and 20 per cent of the water that would be required by a conventional building, and results in immediate payback since there was very little cost premium for the mechanical and electrical systems.

**Community Involvement and Voluntarism:
The Human Side of Citizenship**

There is a tight weave between the work and the philanthropy in which members of the firm are involved. An immersive approach to social issues is backed up by an office culture that encourages and rewards voluntarism, with the inevitable result that 'architecture as citizenship' becomes a matter of personal passion. The partners share the view that voluntarism gives architects a direct insight into the everyday lives and challenges of the clients they serve.

An early example: the office-initiated volunteer programme at Belmont House serving meals to clients was instructive to an understanding of difficulties facing the frail elderly. Its contemporary counterpart is a breakfast organised twice a month at CAMH out of the new drug addiction building, where employees prepare eggs and pancakes for addiction outpatients.[5]

Individuals in the firm follow their own interests in philanthropic activities, in roles as diverse as President of Environmental Defence Canada, to board membership of the Toronto Construction Association and not-for-profit housing associations, advisory board participation for

International Trade Canada and membership on Toronto and Vaughan Design Review Panels. One partner raises money for the University of Toronto's Daniels Faculty of Architecture, Landscape and Design and client Ronald McDonald House Toronto; another received a prestigious citizenship award for contributions to enabling young people with disabilities.

The result is a remarkable legacy of contribution for a mid-sized architectural firm, and a successful experiment in fostering empathetic design through holistic architectural practise. This unusual level of social engagement seems to foster a very practical ability to connect issues to the way we live and express social values through building that is perhaps at the heart of Montgomery Sisam's particular brand of architectural citizenship.

Issues loop meaningfully into the way buildings are conceived, at the level of system, everyday use and detail. An unusually understated paradigm for contemporary architecture typically driven by novelty, but one that sits nicely within its most humanistic aspirations and its finest moments as a problem-solving art tailored to the considerable problems of our time.

the architecture of care
bruce kuwabara

Amalgam

From a global perspective, Canada is a relatively young country in which architects have almost always been inspired by oscillating influences between external precedents and models, and their particular responses to local, regional climate, programmes and sites. In other words, the best architecture produced in Canada has played with formal archetypes adapted to local circumstances and context.

Montgomery Sisam Architects occupy a very interesting position in history, with founding partners who, as baby boomers, were students during the spread of modern architecture. This was a moment when architectural education began to change and open up to a broader range of concerns and interests coincident with changes of values in society as a whole. Their architectural education broadened the base of the discipline from one of formal consistency, integrity and technical development to one that engaged more complex contemporary issues around how we live.

As one looks at the body of work of a firm which has successfully transitioned from the original two partners to the current group of seven, it becomes an interesting challenge to track the ideas that form the core of their body of work. The firm has evolved from making sensible, careful buildings related to healthcare programmes, to buildings of greater complexity, plasticity and public visibility and impact. At the same time, the broader base of leadership has allowed the firm to engage in the complex and challenging world

of public-private partnerships for the delivery of healthcare, academic, and even residential buildings, sponsored and managed by government and financed, constructed, maintained and operated by the private sector.

I would argue that this transformation and adaptation of building typologies remains critically important as a generative strategy for the architecture produced by Montgomery Sisam Architects. I would also suggest that the level of care and understanding that underpins the body of their work represents a substantial contribution to the built environment, particularly in relation to healthcare.

Typology

Every building is a type. Typology is a method of classification and identification of species and, in architecture, building types.

A series of buildings that Montgomery Sisam has designed for long term care demonstrates an evolving manipulation and transformation of the typologies of healthcare. Through rigorous planning and design, they have managed to re-shape the environments of health and wellbeing, an extraordinary accomplishment given the restrictions of budgets and the efficiency metrics in the field.

The place-making aspirations of the projects, and the insistence on developing simple elements—porches, windows, lounges, doorways, common rooms and stairs— reflects a persistent idealism that is searching to restate the

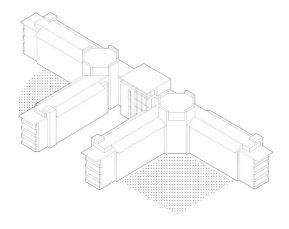

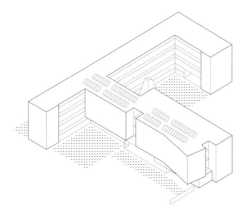

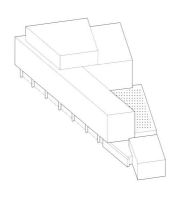

LEFT **The Cardinal Ambrozic Houses of Providence.**

MIDDLE **Ronald McDonald House Toronto.**

RIGHT **The Arts and Administration Building, University of Toronto at Scarborough.**

1. Montgomery Sisam Architects in a joint venture with Kuwabara Payne McKenna Blumberg Architects.

vernacular against the reduction of architecture to equations of form and function.

The resulting buildings embody careful thinking and knowledge of buildings as types, creating new ensembles that form and enclose outdoor landscaped spaces whether they are streets, entrances or garden courts.

Walls

Wall building types that are generally long and narrow are one of the consistent motifs in Montgomery Sisam's body of work, primarily because of the need to provide residential accommodation in healthcare programmes. They have manipulated and explored wall typologies and developed a range of strategies that have transformed the ways in which walls can create a sense of place both inside and outside of their buildings.

The Cardinal Ambrozic Houses of Providence is exemplary as a complex of connected wall buildings, which provide residential accommodation for long term care residents.[1] The development of the building complex and site carefully orchestrates the formation of spaces for arrival, gathering and communal life with the development of wings of repetitive rooms integrated in a house-like format. The attention to materials and detailing manages to sustain a high level of quality over the complete hierarchy of spaces from the individual room to the halls, the lobbies and to the garden and arrival courts.

The use of brick to build walls is careful in its coursing and proportions that allows for the identification of individual windows and rooms within an overall building composition. Significantly, the use of masonry elucidates the building as a work that refers to vernacular masonry construction, while offering something that is transformative in re-shaping healthcare building types.

The placement of wall buildings for Ronald McDonald House Toronto, reinforces the enclosure of Henry Street while simultaneously forming three courtyards. The plan also skilfully establishes two entrances on a through-block site accommodating parking and ground floor lounges and dining areas.

Within the overall organisation of built form on an irregular site, every opportunity has been taken to make urban architecture. Whereas the Houses of Providence express an idealisation of a plan for long term care, Ronald McDonald House Toronto demonstrates a developed dexterity to create a nimble, flexible architecture that strengthens the urban fabric and creates liveable public and communal spaces.

Blocks

Blocks are deeper and generally more nuclear as formed objects of architecture. Montgomery Sisam have deployed blocks in several projects, but always with a view to transforming the building type to be more engaged with its surrounding context, and making the ground floors of the buildings more interactive with the exterior landscape.

The Holland Bloorview Kids Rehabilitation Hospital strategically uses a wall and a block connected to each other to form an L that creates a generous arrival court and entrance sequence.[2] The need to be responsive to the low scale and heights of existing residential buildings led the architects to create a dramatic sloped roof which decreases the height of the wing to relate to existing residences across the street. The block and the taller end of the wall are set deeper on the site with views overlooking a wooded ravine.

The L footprint of the conjoined types also sets up a main entrance and drop-off within an ample forecourt with generous canopies, offering flexibility for a wide range of users and modes of transport.

The block accommodates many of the larger programme elements such as the gymnasium and an auditorium. The development of the section of the block creates opportunities to see into the programme areas for rehabilitation. Full of light and views of the ravine, the block stabilises the building on the site and establishes a strong face, set well back from the street.

The use of zinc cladding unifies the dynamic wall and the anchoring block as one ensemble, while keeping the overall weight of the scheme as light as possible.

As a building that is sited in front of the iconic Scarborough College (now the University of Toronto at Scarborough) designed by the renowned Australian modernist architect, John Andrews, in the 1960s, the Arts and Administration Building is a deceptively simple block, shaped by a series of responses to the site while generating new relationships to lines of movement and the surrounding landscape.

The virtual outline of the block is well-defined and set within the overall master plan for this important modern campus.

The building occupies the full site and clearly defines its edges as a building block. The massing strategy is a more complex development that can been interpreted as an erosion of a large virtual block with a higher portion overlooking the podium and its green roof.

The use of masonry rather than Andrews' exposed concrete resets the tone of the campus, suggesting a shift towards an academic world that is more integrated with the city. Buff brick is developed as a masking surface that is cut and composed selectively to achieve greater openness and to express a larger more public scale, particularly on the main entrance approach.

On both of the long sides of the block, the building reinforces strong lines of pedestrian movement. On the west side, the elevation of the building expresses larger scale gestures while on the east side, a long low steel and glass canopy provides weather protection for pedestrians. On the ground floor there is a space that cuts across the building, connecting both sides. This space double-functions as a breakout area for the auditorium. The architecture establishes a conversation well beyond the accommodation of a complex programme mix on a singular site to speak about issues of an urbanising campus in a contemporary world.

Pavilions

Pavilions are generally free-standing objects. Montgomery Sisam, however, have used the pavilion typology to create apparently free-standing structures that have their own identity as material objects but are also well integrated and connected to their sites and surroundings.

The genius of the project for the Toronto Botanical Garden is how the new architecture simplifies in an astonishing way the whole arrival sequence into this complex of buildings within a civic garden setting. By removing parts of the existing building and an awkward system of level changes at the entrance, the site was edited and cleared for a new retail pavilion, which has the iconography of a glass house. The entrance sequence is welcoming, accessible, greatly enhanced and re-connected to the existing building.

The pavilion stands as a volume in front of the existing buildings. This placement creates a series of gardens and landscaped areas around it that integrate architecture and landscape in a transformative way, creating a series of smaller spaces of special identity related to didactic gardens and outdoor spaces for education.

The elemental pavilion for the Island Yacht Club is carefully sited to establish a frontal relationship and porch to the water and setting sun. Two rectangular clerestory monitors punctuate the roof line to bring light deeper into the space, establishing the pavilion as a variety of tableaux of social settings for gathering, socialising and dining. The building addresses the arrival dock creating a series of layers of landscape upon approach. In this sense, the object becomes one more layer in the landscape. The order of the building is rigorous and simple, relying as

2. Montgomery Sisam Architects in a joint venture with Stantec Architecture.

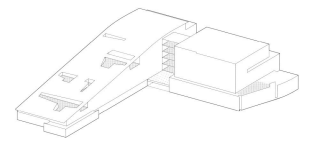 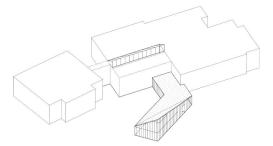 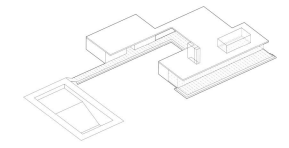

LEFT **Holland Bloorview Kids Rehabilitation Hospital.**

MIDDLE **The George and Kathy Dembroski Centre for Horticulture at the Toronto Botanical Garden.**

RIGHT **Island Yacht Club.**

much on rhythm and proportion as on the use of wood as a construction material.

But even this pavilion is engaged with secondary buildings to create smaller courtyards on the back side of what appears to be a free-standing object.

Care

Ten years ago, my father who was almost 92, was staying at a long term care facility in Hamilton. My sister called to tell me to come as quickly as I could because my father's health had greatly deteriorated. When I arrived at the facility, I remember that the building was modest in scale, and residential in quality.

My father's room was simple, with large windows and views of the sky. It was peaceful and full of natural light. My father was not conscious, so I knelt close to his side to let him know that I was there. All I could hear was his shallow breathing.

My sister and I retreated to the lobby to embrace and cry because we both knew that he wasn't going to make it. I left and returned home only to pick up a message from my sister telling me that my father had passed away. She told me that my father had been hanging on, waiting for me to show up so that we could have that final moment before he left us.

When I later realised that the building had been designed by Montgomery Sisam Architects, I wrote to the architects

to tell them how much I appreciated the ways in which the building supported the dignity of my family and our grieving at such a difficult time.

Architecture anticipates and supports real life experience. At moments like this, architecture is not so much about the composition of facades, nor the quality of materials and details. At my father's care home, I just had the sense of being in a place that had been carefully designed by people who, through their understanding of what happens in such situations, had created a supportive environment.

I felt then, as I do now, that the work of Montgomery Sisam Architects is based on careful observation of human experience, and ultimately, about the role of architecture as a supporting partner in our lives. Their work is about care in design and attention to the issues that matter.

light and air

light and air

What slice of the sun does your building have?
Wallace Stevens

Of the elements of a room, the window is the most marvellous.
Louis Kahn

An Early Experience

In the early days of our practice we were given the opportunity to do alterations and additions to existing long term care facilities for the frail elderly. It goes without saying that, at that stage of our practice, we had very little experience in designing and constructing any building type let alone the more specialised and complex buildings for healthcare. This opportunity, although serendipitous, profoundly affected the direction of our work to come.

These existing long term care facilities from the 1950s and 60s were built with an overarching concern for efficiency and operational economy. Based on a medical model of healthcare planning, they resulted in very spare barracks-like settings. Any kind of amenity or comfort was offered begrudgingly as a sense of place or the quality of resident experience was not part of the idea. Whereas these kinds of efficiencies might have been marginally appropriate for schools and community buildings, they were clearly not acceptable in the seniors' homes where frail elderly people were confined 24 hours a day.

Upon entering any one of these existing long term care facilities, one experienced a sort of sensory meltdown—bad smells, glaring institutional lighting and a material palette that would be expected in a hospital that had gone through too many budget cuts. When leaving one's bedroom, a resident could look down the corridor one way and see a solid fire exit door and look the other way and see an

obtrusive nurses' station with its wall of nurse call panels, serving as a highly visible reminder of the resident's medical needs in case they might have forgotten why they were there. In addition to all this, ceilings were generally acoustic tile and all at the same height; the social spaces were acknowledged only by a marked increase in the number of fluorescent ceiling fixtures. Real private space was virtually non-existent, privacy curtains notwithstanding. The lack of hierarchy and sameness to this environment made way-finding not only difficult for the sometimes confused residents, but also for the visitor.

BELOW **Ontario long term care facility circa 1975.**

OPPOSITE LEFT **Cambridge, UK.**

OPPOSITE MIDDLE **Fresnal Square—the outer segment (in fact each segment) contains the same area as the middle square.**

OPPOSITE RIGHT **A more dignified hospital model. Royal Chelsea Hospital 1692 designed by Sir Christopher Wren.**

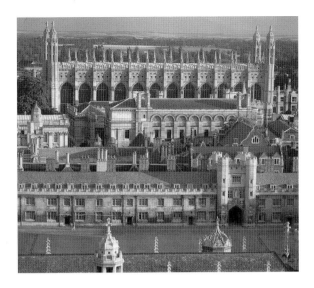
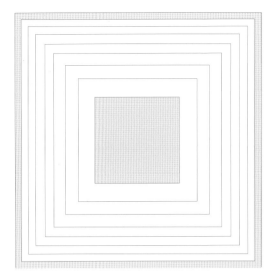

All of this was bad enough, but the recollection of these facilities that stands out above all others was the complete lack of engagement with the outdoors. These facilities were often situated on beautiful properties, whose beauty became a distant memory upon entering the institutionalised, clinically focused and isolating environment of the facility. One felt a palpable feeling of relief upon re-entering the outside world, a feeling the residents seldom got to experience.

If these facilities were what the experts of the time thought appropriate, then perhaps our inexperience, our naivety and our singular desire not to end up in such a place urged us to imagine a new paradigm for this building type; a paradigm with ideas more rooted in the notion of normalcy and of home, which was after all where these residents had come from. This motivation was further informed by precedents of collective homes such as monasteries and earlier more dignified hospital models as well as the late nineteenth and early twentieth century TB sanatoria, where the very embrace of light and air was considered the therapy and cure for the disease. These ideas could be seen as part of a cultural and historical continuum, rather than simply as a specific response to technical and functional requirements.

Skinny Buildings

The architectural implications of built form led Sir Leslie Martin, a British architect and Head of the Department of Architecture at the University of Cambridge, to form the Centre for Land Use and Built Form Studies (now the Martin Centre) in 1967. Martin and his colleagues wanted to show how particular built forms could mitigate the impact of higher densities. To that end they were concerned about the potential of built form to create a sense of place and to optimise the quality of exterior space created by the building footprint.

A seminal diagram for their research was the Fresnal Square. This diagram and its built form implication has had a profound influence on our approach to the disposition of built form. In the Fresnal Square, the outer segment (in fact each segment) contains the same area as the middle square. If one was to imagine the full square as a city block, and the two extremes as buildings, one could suggest some qualitative differences between the two. The perimeter building would be street related, with a shallow floor plate optimising access to light and air. The outdoor space in the centre has the potential to be a garden court or outdoor room for the block. The central building on the other hand is object-like, not related to the streets, with a deep floor plate and with residual, undefined outdoor space surrounding it.

Martin and his colleagues developed a mantra "think-line not think-blob", the think-line proposition advocating skinny buildings that define the space between. It is not surprising that this research began at Cambridge, a university characterised by skinny buildings creating streets and courts.

The effort to make skinny buildings with a strong connection to the outdoors also has the effect of making them

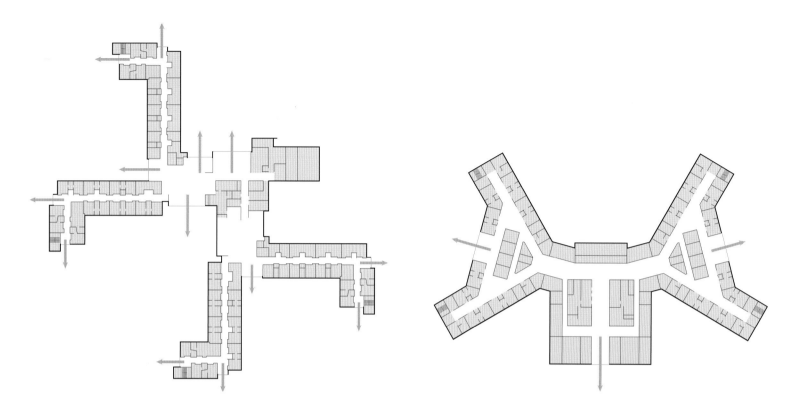

more sustainable. Controlled daylight often makes the use of artificial lighting unnecessary during the daylight hours while shallow floor plates encourage the use of natural ventilation, lowering the reliance on mechanical cooling and ventilation.

Of course, the introduction of sophisticated mechanical systems and the pursuit of strategic functional relationships led to buildings with very deep floor plates often with little regard for natural light or views. This model was particularly evident in the field of healthcare buildings where complex logistics and clinical adjacency requirements held sway over patient experience.

However, recent clinical studies in healthcare settings have shown the healing benefits of both access to daylight and views to natural environments. This connection to the outdoors has a more social or cultural base to offset the necessary, but often prevailing functional, technical and safety demands for healthcare. In the nineteenth century, Florence Nightingale advocated the use of narrow pavilion

buildings to allow maximum cross-ventilation and sunlight for medical reasons.

She says in her diary of 1860, "I mention from experience, as quite perceptible in promoting recovery, the being able to see out of a window, instead of looking against a dead wall; the bright colours of flowers, the being able to read in bed by the light of a window close to the bed head. It is generally said the effect is upon the mind. Perhaps so, but it is no less upon the body on that account...."

In spite of the introduction of sophisticated mechanical systems allowing for larger floor plates, Nightingale's concerns are re-emerging over 100 years after her death as the likelihood of getting sick from a stay at a hospital becomes more and more common. Our work in the field of healthcare has, to the extent possible, encouraged the typology of skinny buildings to maximise access to daylight, views and fresh air for residents and patients. This typology has also facilitated the creation of gardens or outdoor

LEFT **Plan A, a building which encourages the connection of public space to the outdoors and defines a series of garden courts.**

RIGHT **Plan B, more of an object building focussing in on itself without taking into account the value of positive outdoor space or the connection of indoor public space to the outside.**

TOP **Zonnestraal Sanitorium Hilversum, The Netherlands, 1931, designed by Johannes Duiker.**

BOTTOM **A detail from the Nolli Plan of Rome 1768.**

rooms defined and engaged by this built form and used by patients, staff and visitors.

Working the Plan

In 1768 the architect Giambattista Nolli drew a map of Rome on which he blackened in the private spaces and left white the extensive network of streets, squares, parks and even some interior semi-public spaces such as churches, baths, town halls and markets. The Nolli Plan was the precursor of what we now call figure ground plans which provide a compelling way to represent in two dimensions the spatial qualities and sense of place or placelessness of different urban forms. The nature of the figure ground plan encourages the consideration of place as opposed to object as the essence of the plan. Typically, figure ground plans are used to examine a proposed building in its urban context.

We have also used the technique of the figure ground plan within the building footprint to examine the hierarchy and continuity of public spaces and their engagement with the outdoors. The two plans illustrated show, on the one hand, a building which encourages the connection of public space to the outdoors and defines a series of garden courts (Plan A) and, on the other hand, a plan which is quite internalised, leaving only residual outdoor space (Plan B). Plan B is more of an object building focusing in on itself, without taking into account the value of positive outdoor space, or the value of allowing the internal public space more opportunities for access to daylight, views and air.

The appropriate hierarchy and disposition of public space within the plan is at the root of a building's engagement with exterior places and is significant in creating a context for orientation. We have developed strategies such as using single-loaded corridors (more like galleries or promenade decks), locating elevators where there is a view to the outdoors and creating communal rooms with a double aspect, all in an effort to allow the public spaces of the building to breathe light and air. Our design for the accommodation of 81 families at the new Ronald McDonald House in Toronto reflects this approach. In keeping with the design theme of a house in a garden in the city, outdoor recreational garden courts and their engagement with the home's public space are integral to the building's design, offering respite from the experiences of a stressful hospital environment.

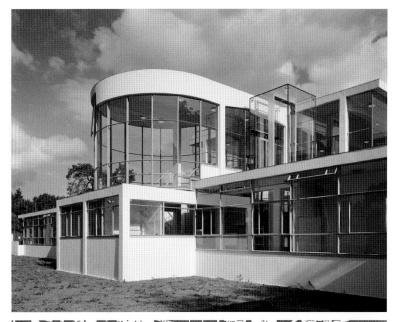

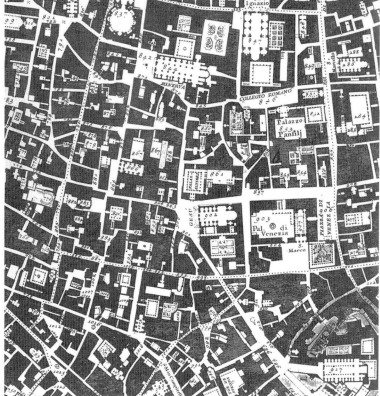

the john c and sally horsfall eaton ambulatory care centre, st john's rehab hospital
2010

BELOW Isometric drawing highlighting the two-storey concourse with its relationship to the therapy court and the rehabilitation pool and gyms.

OPPOSITE New central canopy-covered entrance.

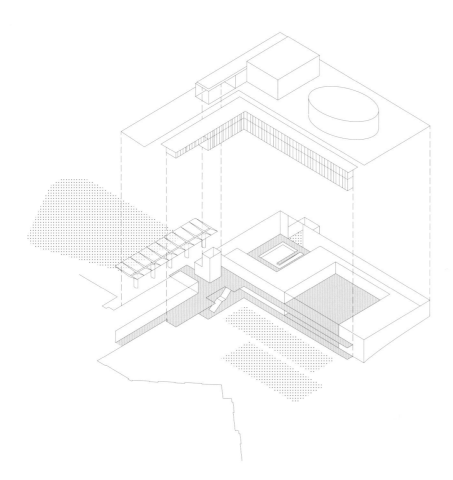

The Ambulatory Care Centre addition to St John's Rehab Hospital sets an example for a more holistic idea about health; one that includes comfort and wellbeing. The facility is designed to advance St John's mission to rebuild the lives of adults recovering from life-changing illness or injury by creating a bright, comfortable setting for individualised rehabilitation programmes focused on the whole person.

The new Ambulatory Care Centre consists of a two-storey 4,700 m² addition to the existing hospital on a treed 9.5 hectare site in North Toronto. The hospital was originally owned and operated by the Sisters of St John the Divine who purchased the property in the 1930s to build a convalescent hospital that could enjoy the benefits of the rural surroundings. Since that time the city has filled in around the hospital, but the large park-like site has been largely preserved. It is adjacent to a branch of Toronto's vast ravine system, which has also been preserved and rehabilitated to become a precious natural ecosystem within the city.

The addition consists of two large rehabilitation gyms and associated clinical offices, a new therapy pool, and a new central canopy-covered entrance for the hospital. The overall project also includes a relocation of the loading dock so as to conceal it from view, as well as the reinstatement of the original entry court which is on axis with the existing tree-lined entry drive.

The programmed spaces in this addition are flexible and adaptable, providing a robust approach to 'future proofing'. The primary circulation defines a new garden

LEFT **The two-storey concourse and stairs.**

RIGHT AND OPPOSITE TOP **The therapy pool with ample natural light creates a calming environment for rehabilitation.**

OPPOSITE BOTTOM **Section through the main entrance.**

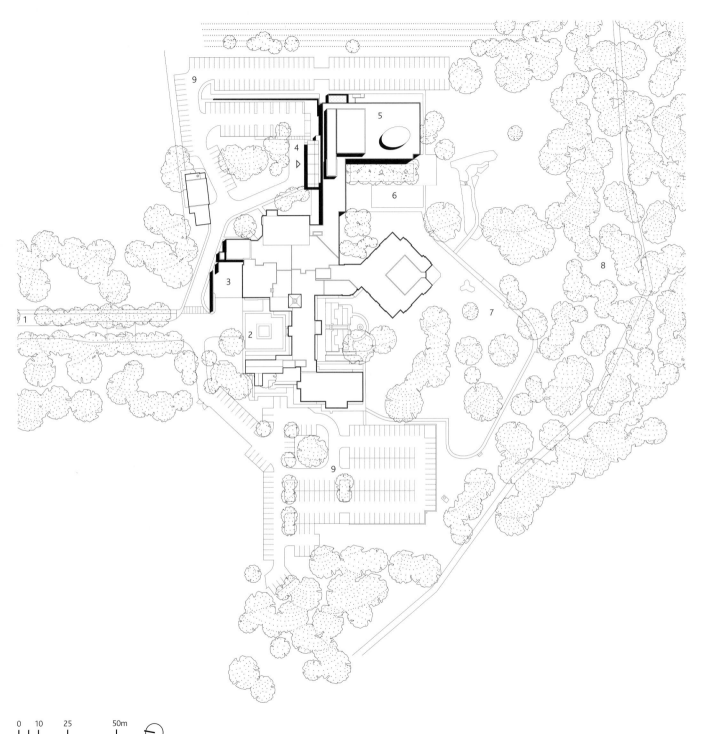

1. entry drive
2. heritage court
3. loading dock
4. main entrance
5. addition
6. therapy court
7. landscaped grounds
8. ravine
9. parking

0   10   25   50m

OPPOSITE Site plan.

LEFT View from the upper concourse through to the therapy court and ravine beyond.

RIGHT Double-height space with clerestory monitor at the main entrance.

← Horsfall Eaton Wing   → Grasett Hall   → Scadding Wing
                                            Administration
← Agnew Wing   → Cafeteria ⑪   → Beatty Wing
   Inpatients

LEFT View from the upper rehabilitation gym through the concourse to the therapy court.

OPPOSITE The therapy court with the daylit concourses providing an ideal setting for patients to regain their mobility and confidence.

court in a two-storey L-shaped arrangement, allowing natural light into the public, office and rehab care spaces. Single-loaded concourses provide views into the therapy court and the landscaped grounds beyond as well as an ideal setting for patients to regain their mobility and confidence. A prominent stair articulates the change in grade from north to south, assisting with way-finding by providing a visual connection between the two levels.

The Ambulatory Care Centre addition brings a new vitality and sense of place to the hospital by reconnecting the hospital to its remarkable surroundings and reviving the opportunity for nature to play a role in the healing process.

This project was completed as a joint venture between Montgomery Sisam Architects and Farrow Partnership Architects.

OPPOSITE The main entrance on McCaul Street.

BELOW Isometric drawing highlighting the
public spaces of the home including a series of
single-loaded corridors overlooking the gardens.

ronald mcdonald house toronto
2011

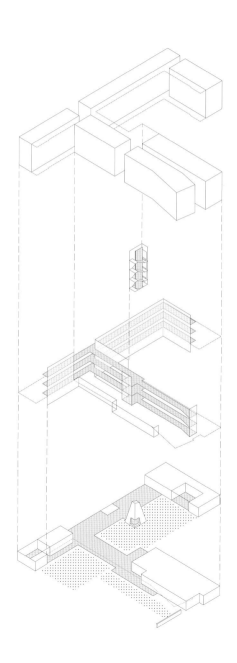

Supported entirely by fundraising and volunteers, Ronald McDonald House provides a 'home away from home' for out-of-town families with seriously ill children. The nearby world-renowned Hospital for Sick Children draws families from across Canada and around the world. Notwithstanding the special needs of the children, the new House is designed to encourage a sense of normalcy for the children and their families, providing an environment where 'kids can be kids' to the fullest extent possible. For these out-of-town families, Ronald McDonald House aims to create a place of comfort, security and refuge. The new four-storey House is designed to accommodate 81 families, making it the largest in the world. The programme includes 66 single-room family suites, 15 two-bedroom family suites, a house manager's suite

and communal facilities including living, dining and kitchen areas as well as administrative and support spaces. The House also includes a unique one-room school for children of different ages and abilities. The average length of stay at the House is 30 days but it can be as long as a year. Through an integrated design process and detailed energy modelling, strategies were developed to create a healthy and energy efficient building that targets a LEED® Gold rating.

The primary architectural idea was to provide a "house in a garden in the city". The disposition of the building on the site creates a series of three landscaped garden courts. The front court is a linear walled garden with a fountain adjacent to the main entry lobby muffling the sounds of the city upon entering the garden. The south court is a quiet contemplative green

OPPOSITE **Communal kitchen and dining area with views both to Henry Street and the garden court.**

LEFT **Entry to the indoor play pavilion.**

RIGHT **Indoor play pavilion.**

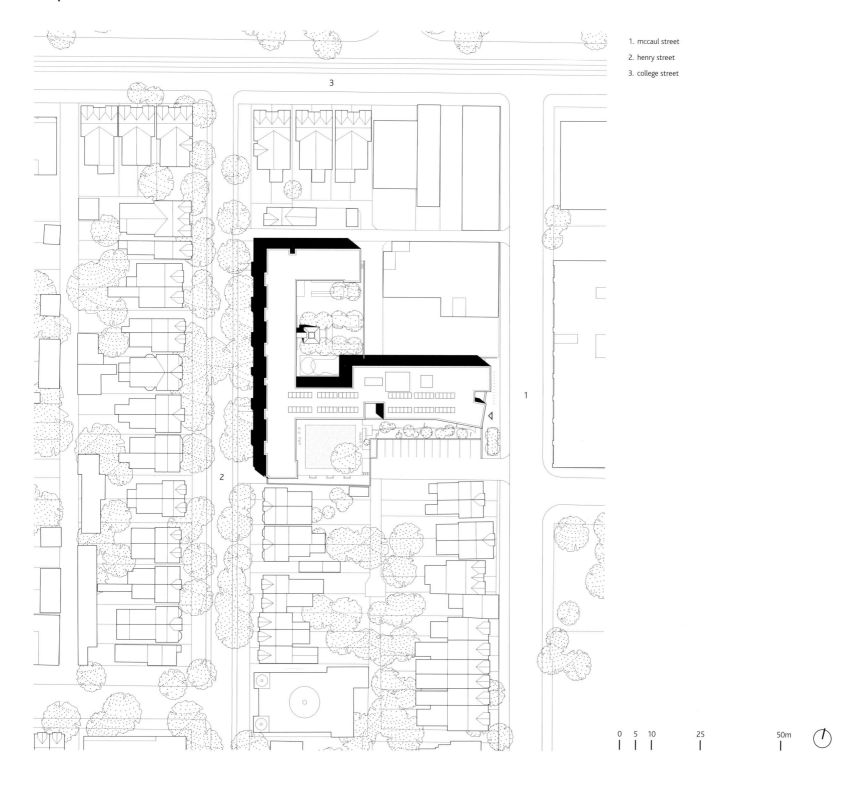

1. mccaul street
2. henry street
3. college street

0 5 10   25   50m

OPPOSITE **Site plan.**

LEFT **Two-bedroom family suite.**

RIGHT **Bed area in typical single-room family suite.**

bordered by a paved walkway. The north court is more active with various play areas and an outdoor dining area. An indoor play pavilion is the central focus of this court. The school, living, kitchen and dining spaces actively use the garden courts. The bright kitchen, looking out onto Henry Street, provides a number of cooking and clean-up stations open to a dining area which, in turn, provides residents the opportunity to be together or alone overlooking the garden court.

On the upper levels, the corridors leading to the bedrooms overlook the gardens providing not only daylight and view but additional sitting spaces close to the family suites where the children are sleeping. The elevator lobby on all floors is open to a south view to provide both daylight and orientation.

Henry Street has some fine Victorian houses and possesses an excellent canopy of mature street trees. The new largely brick building repairs the street wall (the site was previously a parking lot) along Henry Street and responds to the order of the adjacent houses. Domestic functions are gathered along the residential street with living, dining and kitchens at grade and bedrooms on the floors above.

TOP **View from in front of the reception desk towards the large aquarium and main living room.**

BOTTOM **View from a typical bedroom corridor to the north court and the indoor play pavilion.**

OPPOSITE **Ground floor plan.**

1. main entrance
2. henry street entrance
3. house manager's entrance
4. active play court
5. south lawn
6. linear entry garden
7. administration
8. living room
9. teen lounge
10. kitchen/dining
11. indoor play pavilion
12. school
13. receiving

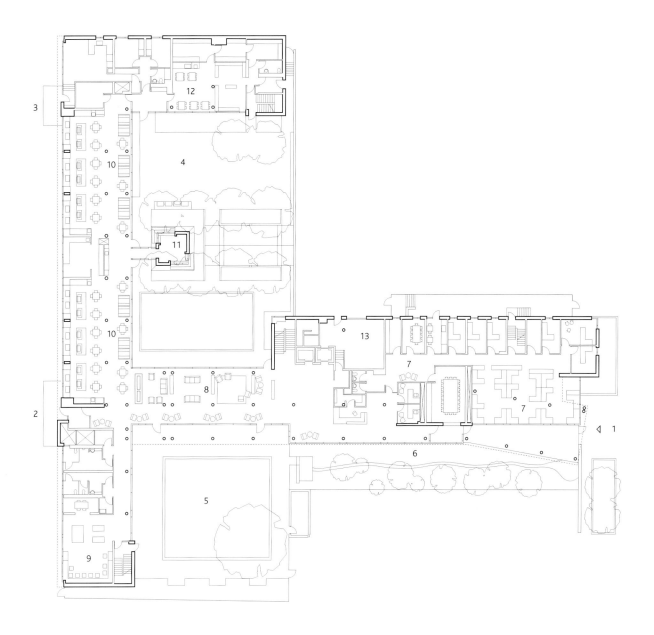

LEFT The south court with the linear entry garden beyond.

OPPOSITE Bedroom corridors in the early evening.

the bob rumball home for the deaf
2006

BELOW Isometric drawing highlighting the public areas of the home and the volumes created by the distinctive metal roofs.

OPPOSITE The home, with the chapel to the right, on a winter evening.

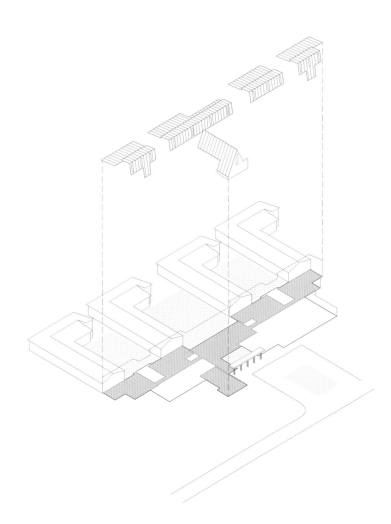

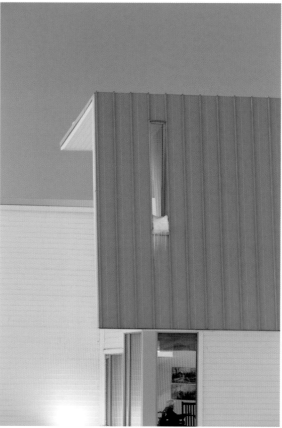

The Bob Rumball Home for the Deaf long term care centre supports the client's mission of housing and serving deaf seniors by creating a unique setting that preserves deaf culture, language and heritage and promotes the residents' right to self-determination and autonomy, ensuring that deaf seniors can thrive as part of a vibrant community.

This long term care centre is the only one of its kind in Canada. The home accommodates 64 residents in four houses on a picturesque park-like setting overlooking Lake Simcoe, Ontario. The programme includes a multipurpose room and chapel for use both by residents and the local deaf community. Comprising a collection of wood clad volumes, the home's design makes reference to the lakeside cottages that are characteristic of the area, creating a gentle rapport with the surrounding

landscape. In summer the white wood volumes with their silver metal roofs contrast with the surrounding lush green landscape while in winter they blend with the snow covered surrounds.

The design is focused around facilitating communication for the occupants. Taking advantage of the 3.2 hectare lot, the home is developed over one level with a variety of double-height spaces. The design is conducive to seniors who depend on a visually oriented environment by providing diffuse light from clerestory windows and skylights to eliminate harsh shadows and silhouettes. The communal spaces such as the dining, lounge and activity areas are designed as contiguous open space (rather than separate rooms) to allow for long sight lines that assist residents with communication by

OPPOSITE LEFT **Entry court and canopy.**

OPPOSITE RIGHT **Corner window and skylight window in the roof.**

BELOW **Interior of the chapel.**

signing as well as providing comfortable and spacious areas for residents to congregate.

Within the intimate setting of the house, each bedroom entry has a built-in 'memory box' for personal mementos that also provides a visual clue for seniors afflicted with dementia. The bedroom doors have been aligned so that residents have visual contact with their neighbours across the hall, providing comfort to those restricted to their beds.

The disposition of the houses on the site creates a series of residential garden courts that are shared by both bedrooms and communal spaces.

OPPOSITE LEFT **Diffuse light from clerestories and skylights eliminate harsh shadows and silhouettes.**

OPPOSITE RIGHT **Roof and wall detail.**

RIGHT **Site plan.**

1. main entrance
2. house
3. residential garden court

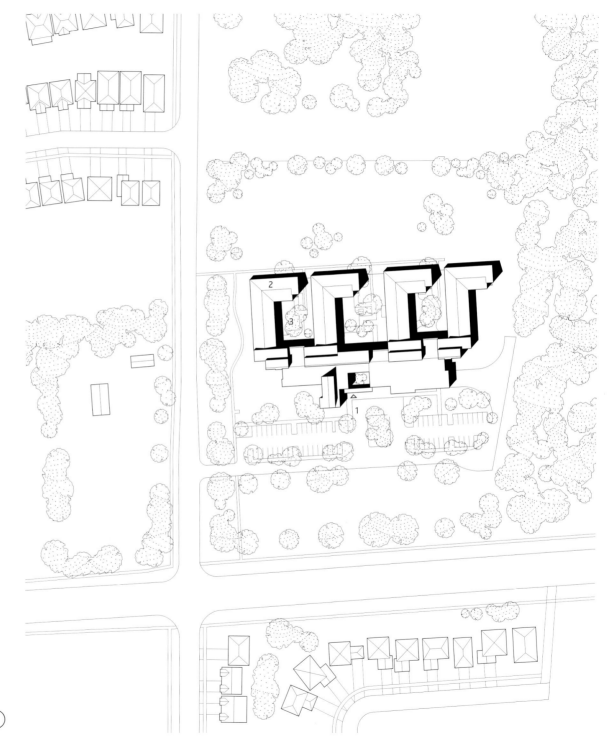

OPPOSITE The main entrance with the chapel on the left.

BELOW Isometric drawing highlighting the core communal spaces of the convent with their articulated roofscape.

convent for the sisterhood
of st john the divine
2005

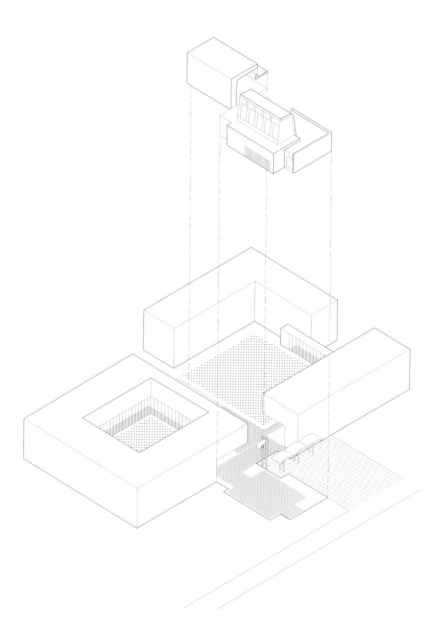

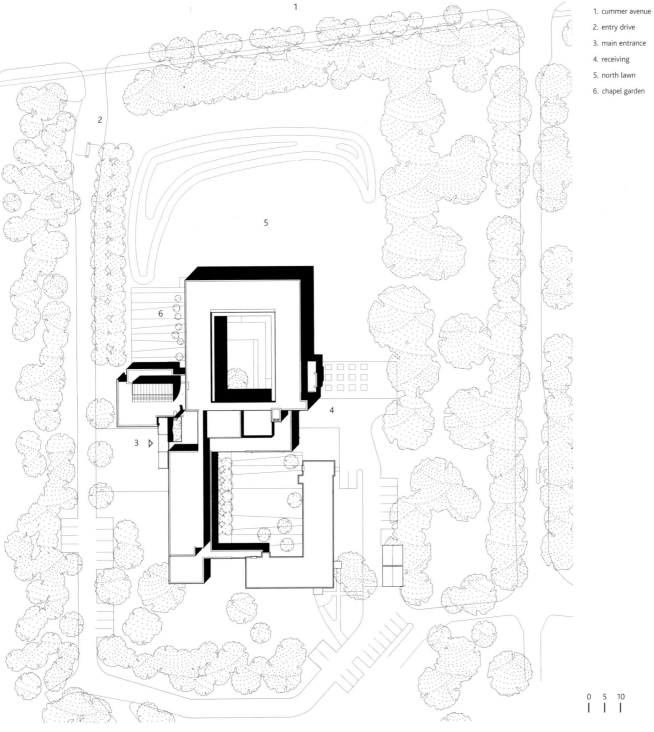

1. cummer avenue
2. entry drive
3. main entrance
4. receiving
5. north lawn
6. chapel garden

0 5 10   25   50m

The Sisterhood of St John the Divine was founded in 1884 as a monastic community for women within the Anglican Church. Today their mission promotes unity, healing and wholeness through prayer, spiritual guidance, hospitality and ministering to those in need. The Sisterhood is a stable community with an active novitiate, committed to a balance of life in which prayer, work, rest and study each have a place and shape the rhythm of the day. As such, the need for a suitable home and a place for quiet contemplation was the driving force behind building this new convent.

Set well back from busy Cummer Avenue in a wooded enclave beside St John's Rehab Hospital in Toronto (founded by the Sisters in 1937), the building is restrained in expression, sitting quietly in its natural setting. The complex consists of simple two-storey brick blocks set in a figure eight pattern accommodating 36 Sisters. The building blocks each enclose private courtyards and incorporate a former nurse's residence which has been converted into a guest house. One courtyard serves as a private residential enclosure for the Sisters, while the other more open courtyard is surrounded by public functions that include a small conference centre, a library, the refectory and the L-shaped guest house. The Sisters' accommodation is designed on two levels around a glazed cloister that surrounds and opens onto the courtyard.

The chapel, community room, refectory, concrete bell tower and timber-framed entrance canopy are each given distinct expression in contrast to the elemental brick blocks with their random pattern of

OPPOSITE **Site plan.**

LEFT **The private residential courtyard for the Sisters.**

RIGHT **Sister exercising in the residential courtyard.**

OVERLEAF **The chapel with its roof monitor and stained glass windows below; Ground floor plan.**

1. reception
2. chapel
3. sister's residence
4. sister's courtyard
5. community room
6. refectory
7. guest house (existing)
8. guest courtyard
9. conference rooms
10. library

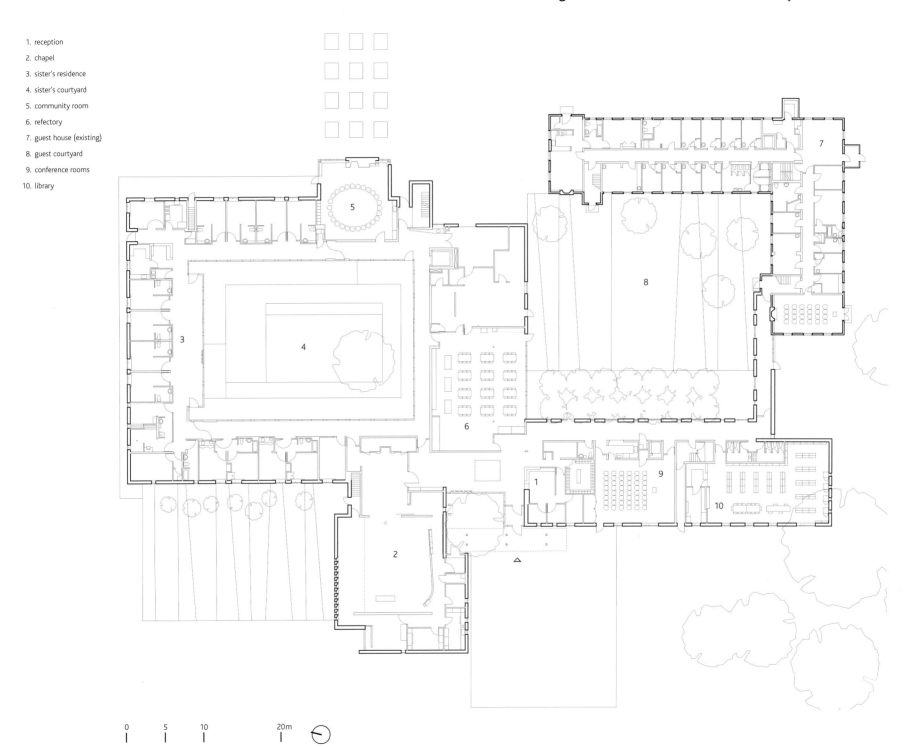

0   5   10   20m

BELOW **The curved zinc roof of the chapel.**

OPPOSITE LEFT **The beech ceiling with north windows.**

OPPOSITE RIGHT **Chapel interior.**

LEFT The main entrance at night.

RIGHT The timber-framed entrance canopy
and concrete bell tower.

OPPOSITE Sisters at prayer.

punched windows. The chapel, the heart of the complex, has a high vaulted ceiling with windows facing north towards the entrance to the site, creating a welcoming beacon. The design for the beech ceiling panels suggests a protective hand folded to gather and contain the light from the north windows. The soft plastered walls reflect stained-glass filtered daylight that illuminates the space. The absence of outward views defines the chapel as a place of prayer and introspection. In contrast, the double-height refectory receives the bright south light and opens out onto the guest courtyard, responding to the shared, communal life of the Sisterhood.

restoration services centre
2007

BELOW Isometric drawing highlighting the
major components of the building.

OPPOSITE View of the Centre from across the
service yard.

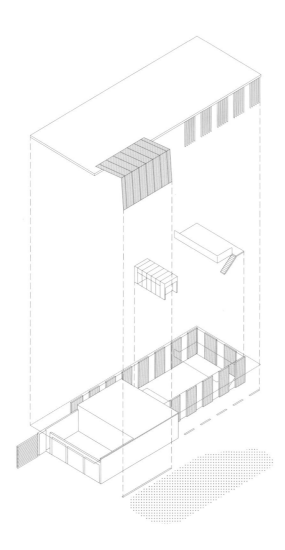

1. entry drive
2. ponds
3. main entrance
4. service yard

0 10 25 50m

The Restoration Services Centre in Vaughan, Ontario responds to the Toronto and Region Conservation Authority's (TRCA) mandate to facilitate a broad understanding of integrated approaches to sustainable living.

The Centre is a part of the 'Living City Campus' selected in 2007 as the location for the World Green Building Council Secretariat. The Living City Campus initiates, inspires, supports and monitors change toward sustainable living. The TRCA recognises the potential impact of the built environment on the approximately 40,000 acres of wilderness area under their stewardship. The Centre provides a prototype of an environmentally responsive built environment that supports the long term viability of urban wilderness settings.

The Restoration Services Centre, the first building in Eastern Canada to be LEED® Platinum certified, supports this mission by using simple, affordable design solutions and materials to drive high sustainability outcomes. The two-storey 1,095 m^2 building comprises offices for management and field personnel that are designed to accommodate large seasonal staff increases; it also includes a workshop, garage, storage space, support spaces and provision for a future greenhouse for the aquatic plant propagation programme.

A careful analysis of the site influenced basic design decisions. The east–west orientation of the building maximises the benefits of north and south exposures. The deep south-facing porch shields the windows from hot summer sun but allows the lower winter sun into the building. Low occupancy areas,

OPPOSITE **Site plan.**

TOP **North wall of the Centre with the entrance to the right.**

BOTTOM **West-facing garage.**

such as the workshop and change rooms, were located at the west end of the building to further shelter the office space from excessive heat gain and harsh afternoon sun. The generous windows and a narrow floor plate of the office space allow for abundant natural light and through-ventilation, reducing the demand for artificial lighting and cooling and ensuring that every employee is within five metres of an operable window. The generous interior volume, bathed in dappled light, provides an ideal setting to germinate aspirations about a more sustainable city.

Within this main double-height space, much of the structure has been left exposed to allow a better understanding of the building's construction and to minimise the use of redundant materials and their attendant costs. Through the use of a ground source heat pump, occupancy and photocell sensors for artificial lighting, heat recovery and passive tempering of fresh air, a high level of energy efficiency was achieved (61 per cent better than the Model National Energy Code). Composting toilets, waterless urinals and ultra low flow faucets and shower heads substantially reduce potable water consumption (80 per cent reduction in potable water consumption compared to the reference building) while displacement air ventilation and low VOC emitting materials contribute to healthy indoor air quality. Non-potable water is sourced from four ponds nearby, significantly reducing demand for the municipally provided potable water. All the storm water collected from the roof and surrounding site is directed to the ponds to compensate. A large wall made from reclaimed bricks marks the building's entrance.

OPPOSITE **The generous windows and narrow floor plate of the office space allow for abundant natural light and through-ventilation.**

LEFT **The deep south-facing porch.**

RIGHT **View of the Centre from across one of the ponds.**

summer house prince edward island
2006

BELOW Isometric drawing highlighting the indoor and outdoor living area of the house surrounding the garden court.

OPPOSITE Summer house with the Gulf of St Lawrence beyond.

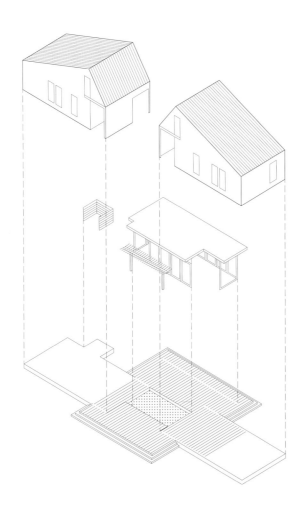

This summer house is located on rolling farmland near Malpeque on the North Shore of Prince Edward Island, looking out over Branders Pond and the Gulf of St Lawrence.

The house is designed to focus views to the seashore, the pond and the surrounding farmland while screening out views of numerous new cottages built up and down the shore.

The house consists of two sloped roof pavilions connected with a glazed link creating a small sheltered garden court between the two pavilions. One pavilion contains the master bedroom, kitchen and a double-height living space. The second pavilion accommodates a small office, three bedrooms (two on a second floor), laundry area, bathroom and an outdoor storage room. The dining space is in the glazed link and has focused views in all four directions. A generous screened outdoor shower is incorporated along the south face of one of the pavilions.

The pavilions and link are narrow (one room deep) to maximise daylight and through-ventilation. Exterior wood decks extend the living space to the outdoors. The house is constructed of standard wood framing with exposed structural wood deck floors and roofs and urethaned plywood partitions. The exterior palette consists of eastern cedar shingles, a metal roof and vinyl-clad windows, all sourced locally.

OPPOSITE Garden court with deck and trellis.

RIGHT Summer house with outdoor shower
and glazed link in the foreground and Branders
Pond beyond.

1. gulf of st lawrence
2. branders pond
3. culivated fields
4. lawn

0 10 25 50m

OPPOSITE Site plan.

LEFT View through the dining area to the garden court and the Gulf of St Lawrence beyond.

RIGHT Double-height space of the living room and kitchen.

economy of means,
generosity of ends

economy of means, generosity of ends

Economy is the art of making the most of life.
George Bernard Shaw

A Matter of Priority

A fixed and often tight building budget is typically seen by architects as an unfortunate reality of the world in which we live. The nature of the work in our office, much of it in service for people with special needs, seems to inevitably bring with it such budgets. As a result, one tries to see the challenge as an opportunity to do more with less, an undertaking that can bring forth some sense of accomplishment in helping clients achieve their objectives. This budget context brings focus— the necessity of establishing what is really important in the project and being very pragmatic about the execution. Often this means keeping things simple and relying on a few strong moves to provide richness in the context of thrift.

When faced with a fixed budget and building programme, there are two variables at play—the area of the building and the cost per unit of area. Naturally, as the area increases, the cost per unit of area (and building quality) diminishes. For us it has become a matter of priority to be extremely efficient in planning to reduce area to allow for a more generous cost per unit of area. This exercise requires an inordinate amount of time, working the plan and its efficiencies, while trying also to maximise the amenity provided through the plan—amenity such as single-loaded corridors, views at end of corridors, etc..

These plan efficiencies free up resources to introduce a few elements that though modest can enrich the project— elements such as the conical skylight for the Sister Margaret Smith Addictions Treatment Centre, or the roof monitor for the Island Yacht Club or simply the act of creating generous window sills for residential occupancy, window sills that can accommodate favourite possessions such as family photographs. This challenge also becomes an exercise to find opportunities reliant on full knowledge of the building code, construction methods and programme efficiencies. Whatever virtuosity there is in this process isn't reflected so much in building expression or a rich material palette but rather in a much more back-room, hidden type of virtuosity. This involves a very collaborative process with clients and consultants that fully respects the clients' priorities while making projects of enduring quality.

Coming to Terms with Vinyl Siding (or its equivalent)[1]

One of the by-products of a tight budget is a diminished range of materials from which to select. This is not the world of sumptuous galleries and museums but rather of inexpensive normative fabric buildings whose significance has less to do with form-making and more to do with creating a sense of place. Vinyl siding is a pretty nasty material but it has the advantages of cost, ease of maintenance and ease of installation, making it very attractive to a cost conscious client.

There are of course precedents for both great buildings and great cities being created from low cost materials. Luis Barragan's iconic houses are essentially planes of stucco in

1. This challenge is discussed with eloquence in *Global City Blues* by Daniel Solomon.

striking colours that create a remarkable sense of place. At a larger scale, the city of St Petersburg, a much admired exemplar of urbanism, is largely a city of yellow stucco with stone trim.

When required to use these materials we arrange them as simple planes to be a background for moments of more energised expression. The Peter D Clark Centre, for example, uses bay windows, chimneys and roof forms to provide a richness of expression while using inexpensive cement board siding as its primary cladding material.

The Centre of Excellence for Integrated Senior Services using stucco and cement board cladding relies on colour, an animated ground floor and shifts in massing to provide relief from the simple punched window planes.

Multivalence

Another strategy for achieving economy in building is to create places that have multiple interpretations of use to exist in concert with one another. This is not to be confused with flexible spaces which are designed to accommodate everything while not being particularly good for any one thing. A multivalent space integrates functions rather than segregating them into separate spaces and can be put to different uses without having to change the space or compromise any of the functions. At Greenwood College School the interior focal point is an atrium that plays multiple roles with equal success. The atrium is a source of natural light and a ventilation 'chimney' for the ground floor while serving as a fly tower associated with the stage used for assemblies and performances. It also incorporates a climbing wall scaling up the four floors of the building. This multivalent place creates a physical setting that responds to many of the unique aspects of the School's curriculum in a way which animates and adds richness to the whole.

The Family Resource Centre at the Holland Bloorview Kids Rehabilitation Hospital functions as a large lobby and waiting area as well as a more informal extension of the Research Library. The Centre also accommodates large receptions and regular concerts.

Another example at a smaller scale is the incorporation of decorative wood trim in the corridor for Belmont seniors' apartments. The trim is at handrail height with a flat top and can be used by residents as a support—a handrail that doesn't look like a typical handrail with all its connotations of a healthcare setting.

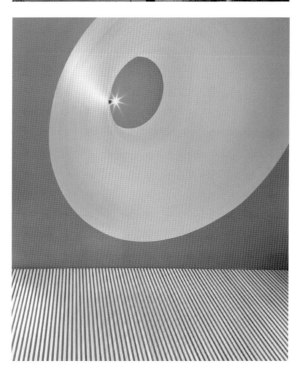

OPPOSITE TOP **St Petersburg, largely a city of stucco with stone trim.**

OPPOSITE BOTTOM **A house by Luis Barragan.**

TOP **The Centre for Excellence in Integrated Seniors Services, Thunder Bay, Ontario.**

MIDDLE **Peter D Clarke Centre, Nepean, Ontario.**

BOTTOM **Conical skylight, Sister Margaret Smith Addiction Treatment Centre, Thunder Bay, Ontario.**

island yacht club
2006

BELOW Isometric drawing highlighting the free-flowing indoor and outdoor public areas with space-defining chimney, glazed screens and roof monitors.

OPPOSITE The clubhouse at night as seen from the front lawn.

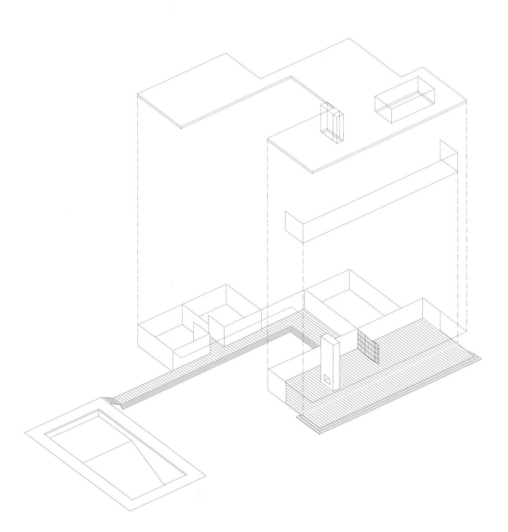

The new building for the Island Yacht Club replaces an older, beloved clubhouse that was destroyed by fire in June 2003. The new building had to fulfil the club's business goals, allowing for future expansion and providing a new identity for the club to help rebuild its image and membership after the devastating effects of the fire. The new clubhouse was rebuilt entirely on the proceeds of the insurance settlement, imposing very tight budget restrictions on the project. The site is only accessible by water, so all material and labour had to arrive by boat and barge.

The resulting structure, built on 60 piles, hovers slightly above the flat, sandy soil of Mugg's Island which forms part of the archipelago of the Toronto Islands with Toronto Harbour on one side and Lake Ontario on the other. It is a natural setting visually isolated from the city yet only minutes away across the water. The programme components of the building are arranged to both define outdoor places and to integrate aspects of

the existing site features: boat slips, lawn, pool and boat yard, in a manner that makes the clubhouse the core of the overall experience of the place.

The building consists of two north–south blocks. The first is a glazed pavilion which overlooks the front lawn and docks and contains public functions that include a dining room, bar, lounge and porch. The second block contains the locker functions.

A court between the two blocks provides a more private outdoor place intended for use by members enjoying the pool. The kitchen connects the two blocks and creates a third side to the pool court. All of the programme components are either connected directly to one another or through exterior covered walkways. An extensive deck system allows for seamless transition from inside to outside.

Both the floor and roof supported by the steel column and beam structure consist of 75 mm tongue and groove planking that forms both the base structure

OPPOSITE The horizontal projection of both the floor and roof.

RIGHT The dining area with views to the front lawn and the moored sailboats.

LEFT **The edge of the lounge with its wood plank roof and joists supported by steel beams.**

RIGHT **The pool court with deck and locker rooms beyond.**

OPPOSITE **The lounge areas with double-sided fireplace.**

1. main entrance
2. front lawn
3. pool court
4. pool

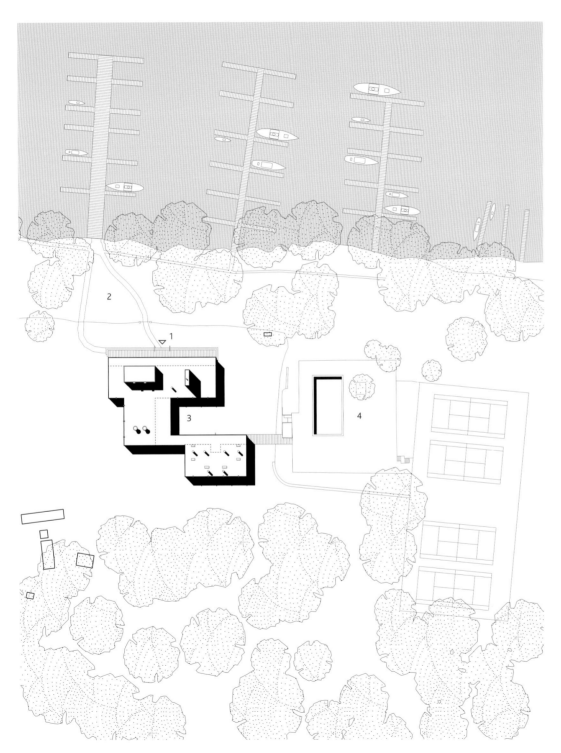

0   5   10   25   50m

and the finished material. The low horizontal plane of the roof ensures the building sits quietly in the flat landscape with minimal visual disruption to the natural beauty of the tall cottonwood trees. Two glazed vertical elements project above the roof plane providing natural ventilation due to the chimney effect, creating varying internal volumes at the fireplace and dining room as well as acting as light beacons easily seen by returning sailors. The building is intended for summer use only and relies on its narrow footprint and extensive opening patio doors to facilitate through-ventilation.

Though permanent, the building nevertheless has visual lightness and transparency. The horizontal projection of both floor and roof remind one of the sheltered deck of a river boat where the limits of enclosure are ambiguous and flexible.

OPPOSITE Site plan.

BELOW The clubhouse from one of the boat slips.

greenwood college school
2003

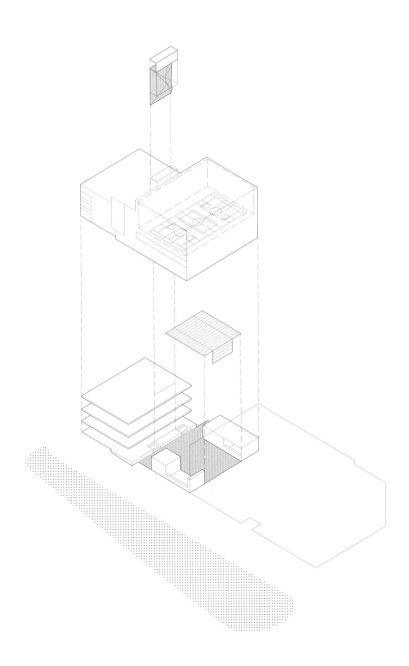

LEFT **The 'lodge'.**

RIGHT **Wiarton stone wall and wood soffit at the main entry.**

OPPOSITE **Site plan.**

Greenwood College School is a co-educational high school with a mandate to develop each student as a whole person with a goal of life-long learning and fostering responsibility. The school redefines the learning environment by integrating its urban Toronto campus with a sister facility (Kilcoo Camp) in the Haliburton Highlands, north of Toronto, where part of the school year's curriculum is taught. Each student is provided with a wireless laptop computer and all classrooms are equipped with interactive whiteboards and control systems.

The 4,181 m² school is designed to accommodate 300 students with 18 classrooms, a large multi-purpose assembly space, a resource centre, a performance theatre and art studio as well as staff offices, gymnasium and cafeteria. The 0.16 hectare site is at a major city intersection and is bounded by both residential and commercial buildings.

The design for the school reuses an existing 1960s office building on the site, wrapping it in a new facade while making a major new addition to the south. The academic and administrative functions are located in the renovated three-storey structure with the gym, some science classrooms and the 'lodge' located in the new section. The lodge is the main meeting area and the hub of student activity. A cedar ceiling and large stone fireplace bring some of the qualities and spirit of the camp facility into the city. Separating the

1. mount pleasant road
2. davisville avenue
3. main entrance
4. renovated office building
5. new addition
6. future addition

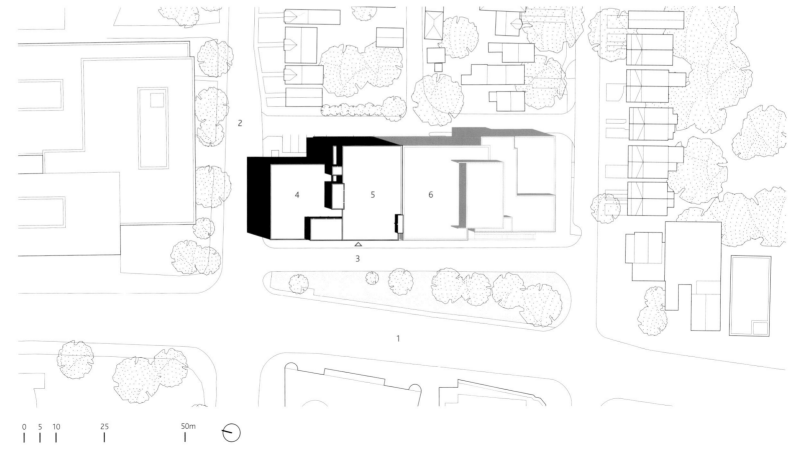

0 5 10   25   50m

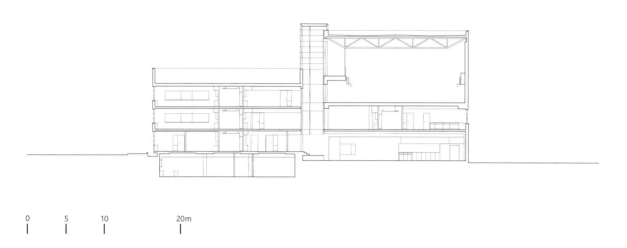

0   5   10   20m

renovated and new building is a central four-storey atrium with a climbing wall on its north face. At the base of the atrium and at one end of the lodge is a platform which serves as both a stage for assemblies and performances as well as a base for the climbing wall. The atrium's central location provides natural light to the interior classrooms and corridors as well as allowing natural ventilation through a chimney effect for the ground floor. The atrium also acts as a fly tower for the stage platform.

The stucco and Wiarton stone facade provides a neutral backdrop for the asymmetrical composition of various window sizes, giving expression to the multiple functions of the interior.

A brick elevator shaft wrapped by a central stair is retained as a totemic element and is exposed to view on the street elevation. A new three-storey glazed corner enclosing this space takes advantage of the school's prominent location on a north–south arterial road by creating a glowing beacon at night and providing a place for banners and displays.

The design demonstrates that a rich and diverse learning environment can be an integral part of the neighbourhood and city fabric. The building contributes to an active street life along the busy arterial road, while, at the same time providing a buffer for the residential streets behind. A new addition to the school, providing specialised programmes and classrooms including a black-box theatre, larger gymnasium and art room is currently in the planning stage.

OPPOSITE The bay windows, Extendicare,
Port Hope.

BELOW Isometric drawing of Extendicare
Port Hope highlighting the 'bridge' of shared
communal space fronting the enclosed garden
courts and serving a pair of houses on each
floor (each house accommodates
32 residents).

extendicare canada
2004

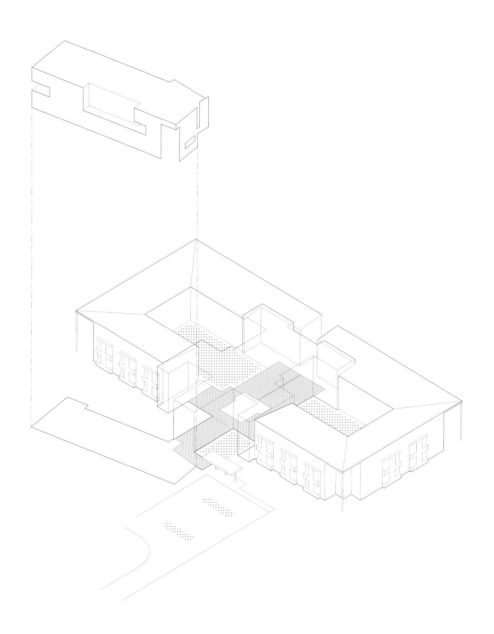

In 2001, the Government of Ontario established a programme to build 20,000 new long term care beds to be constructed according to design guidelines prepared and administered by the Province's Ministry of Health and Long Term Care. Extendicare was awarded licences to construct 11 new homes; our firm was responsible for the delivery of seven of the largest of those homes over a three-year period.

Through an intense and collaborative design process which took advantage of the client's extensive administrative, construction and online nursing experience, functional programmes, key component relationships and prototypical room layouts were developed. This set the framework for the design of homes of different sizes in a variety of locations, all with tight budgets and aggressive schedules.

The tight budget precipitated an examination of plan efficiencies, achieving area reductions that enabled the enhancement of the building finishes in higher profile areas without affecting the overall budget. The area per resident for these homes was an extremely efficient 54 m^2 (typical area per resident is 65 to 70 m^2), making them cost effective both from a capital and operations standpoint. This was achieved without compromising the livability of the new homes that typically have a number of single-loaded corridors and bedrooms that are 15 per cent larger than the Ministry's required room sizes. In some cases building area reduction was achieved through the design of flexible spaces equipped with easy to operate moveable partitions to facilitate multiple functions.

OPPOSITE LEFT **The main entrance of Extendicare, Port Hope.**

OPPOSITE RIGHT **The corner windows providing the corridors with daylight and views out, Extendicare, Port Hope.**

RIGHT **Site plan, Extendicare, Port Hope.**

1. main entrance
2. houses
3. enclosed garden court
4. administration/
   support

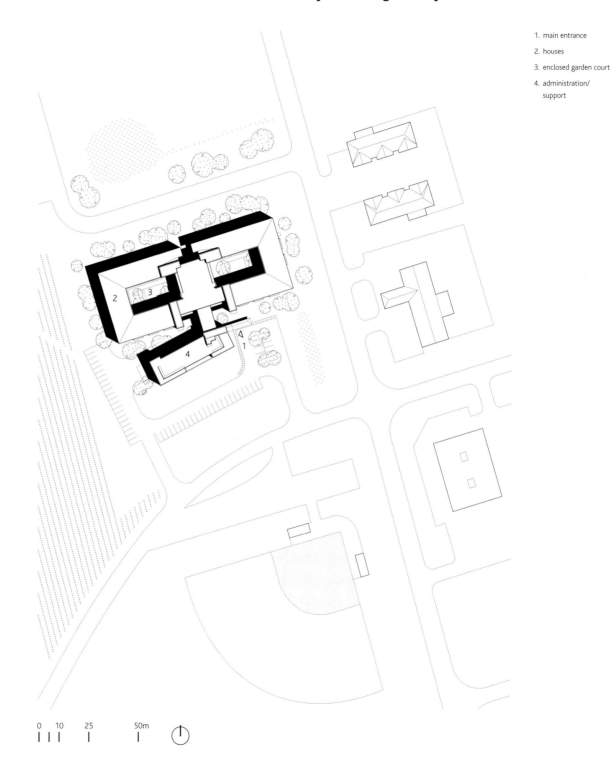

0   10   25   50m

LEFT Extendicare, Rouge Valley. The triple-height lounge area with interior windows providing views from the resident houses.

OPPOSITE LEFT The main entrance, Extendicare, Rouge Valley.

OPPOSITE RIGHT The enclosed court and terraces, Extendicare, Rouge Valley.

The enclosed court typology was developed both for its operational efficiency and to provide safe and secure landscaped gardens on sites that were, in many cases, fringe suburban areas without existing trees or supporting context. Travel distances are reduced for both staff and residents and the extensive corridor glazing provides daylight and views and helps with orientation. The enclosed court typology also allows for a continuous and varied walking loop with no dead ends for residents who have dementia but who retain lots of physical energy.

Design features in the homes include fireplaces, large bedroom windows, outdoor terraces, natural light in the spa bathing area, low windowsills to give residents in wheelchairs good views to the outdoors and 'memory boxes' that house residents' cherished possessions to assist them in recognising their own bedroom entrances.

OPPOSITE McCaul Street facade.

BELOW Isometric drawing highlighting the entrance lobby with its green wall and other reception and lobby areas.

university of toronto st george campus
central examination facility
2008

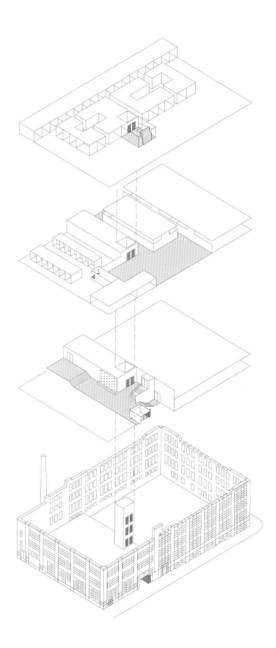

Originally built as a warehouse for the Toronto Board of Education, this 1931 heritage-listed Art Deco building was purchased by the University of Toronto in 2002. The programme for the adaptive reuse of this building incorporates the St George Campus Exam Centre on the first three floors and the relocation of the University's Capital Projects and Facilities and Services Department from their current location to the fourth floor of the building. All this was to be done while preserving, rejuvenating and repairing a significant piece of Toronto's heritage landscape.

The St George Campus Exam Centre is the first dedicated examination facility on campus and provides a supportive environment for exam writing for a range of students including those with special needs. The project accommodates up to 1,000 students and includes two 300-seat exam rooms, three 100-seat exam rooms and a fully accessible centre with specialised exam and testing rooms for students who have mobility, low vision or hearing disabilities. The fourth floor provides 2,200 m² of open work areas and private offices as well as meeting rooms for the Capital Projects and

LEFT The new entrance inserted into the existing building.

RIGHT The straight run stair to the outside.

OPPOSITE The former oversized existing loading bay was converted to a generous entrance lobby, capable of accommodating hundreds of students coming in and out of exams.

TOP AND BOTTOM **Typical exam rooms.**

OPPOSITE **The entrance lobby of the offices for Capital Projects and Facilities and Services.**

Facilities and Services Department. Through the use of more efficient office layouts and standards, the Department occupies 25 per cent less space than they did at the previous location. The majority of the staff are in open office space along the perimeter with private offices and meeting rooms located centrally, borrowing daylight through the open office area.

The alterations to the existing heritage building incorporate many sustainable features including rooftop rainwater/greywater collection, high efficiency lighting and significant improvements to the building envelope. The offices for Capital Projects and Facilities and Services were registered as LEED® Gold CI, the first such ranking for the University of Toronto.

The approach to the adaptive reuse of this building was to maintain the Art Deco warehouse character of the building, restoring existing elements which had deteriorated or been compromised by previous renovations. At the same time, new elements were added using a contemporary but complementary vocabulary.

The approach also took advantage of particular conditions. For example, the oversized existing loading bay, with its generous floor-to-floor height, was converted to the entrance lobby, capable of accommodating hundreds of students coming in and out of exams. A green wall was introduced here to provide a calming and restorative environment while also improving the air quality.

transcending expectations

transcending expectations

I do not see the value in universal truths—a free form does not occupy higher moral ground than a revivalist nineteenth century porch. Instead it is the experience that counts—how we make places rich in evocation; how we translate dignity, sociability and joy into architecture. Julie Eizenberg

Architecture isn't just for special occasions. Koning Eizenberg Architecture

The Hidden Potential of Gross Up

Most building programmes with their accompanying space tables tend to be relatively matter-of-fact and functionally focussed. Any ambitions or aspirations of the programme are usually expressed in the most general of terms. The importance of non-programmed space, typically referred to as "gross up", is seldom recognised in the programme. Circulation space—corridors and stairs—that has the potential of being the life blood of a project is generally a component of gross up. In fact, funding agencies make every effort to reduce gross up.

The great American architect, Louis Khan, once described the characteristics of a stair that would serve everyone, young and old. The stair would have a landing with a seat at a window looking out over the surrounding neighbourhood. He said this window seat was a gesture for an older person wishing to rest part way up the stair. The older person would claim that he or she wanted to sit and admire the view without admitting that they needed to rest. This particular example, in microcosm, reflects an attempt to give people dignity in a way that doesn't draw attention to their physical frailties—that indeed provides a delightful pause for everyone climbing the stair. This whole story, so significant to the human quality of the place happens in the unprogrammed space or gross up, a quantitative element of the building programme.

Corridors in a functional ethos are considered as simply a means of getting somewhere as opposed to being somewhere, rather like collector roads. As discussed under "Light and Air",

we consider the corridor as having the characteristics of a street or gallery, sometimes with views to the outside, with dimensional variety in plan and section, which will transcend the expectation or rather the lack of expectation set out in the quantitative notion of gross up.

In cities, public spaces—streets and squares—are the framework around which everything else is built. The public spaces typically exist before the building fabric fills in. In building programmes it is typically just the opposite, with circulation—a significant portion of the public space—being simply assigned along with duct shafts and wall thicknesses to gross up. This puts great pressure on the architect to correct the inappropriate sense of priorities and redefine the programme meaning in the built form.

BELOW **The Holland Bloorview Kids Rehabilitation Hospital, gallery overlooking the therapeutic pool.**

OPPOSITE TOP **The Cardinal Ambrozic Houses of Providence, room entry.**

OPPOSITE MIDDLE **The Isabel and Arthur Meighen Manor, secure garden court.**

OPPOSITE BOTTOM **The Arts and Administration Building, University of Toronto at Scarborough, classroom corridor overlooking green roof.**

At the Holland Bloorview Kids Rehabilitation Hospital in Toronto, an interior corridor becomes a gallery with places to sit overlooking a therapeutic pool. At the Arts Administration Building at the University of Toronto at Scarborough, a second floor classroom corridor becomes a place itself to sit and wait for classes to begin while overlooking the green roof. At Belmont House Long Term Care Facility in Toronto the elevator lobby on each floor is a lounge with views out over a garden court—a place for residents to sit and watch the comings and goings. Upon getting off the elevator, one is not confronted with a nurses' station, but rather with a view of the world outside.

The House, the Grand Hotel, the Village and the Garden

Our work in the field of healthcare ranging from accommodation of long term care residents and mental health patients to hospitals for rehabilitation and complex continuing care has provided us with the opportunity to question and reconsider some of the long held precepts typical for this work.

Programmes for these facilities are most often based on a medical rather than a residential model. They emphasise what differentiates these residents and patients from the general populace as opposed to what is common between us. As architects we challenged this medical model. Paradigms such as the house, the grand hotel, the village and the garden were useful precedents because they represent places infused with cultural tradition, fond memories and compelling images in contrast to the technical and clinical focus of conventional healthcare facilities.

In the case of long term care residents, their accommodation increasingly constitutes their total physical world. The notion of either village or grand hotel sets an aspirational framework for providing a hierarchy of places, each with a particular character and identity such that the residents have real choice and variety in their living environment. The gathering place according to this notion would be a place that is continuously active and vibrant, a 'town square' (village) or 'salon' (grand hotel) rather than the typical auditorium with its limited use and lack of connectedness to anywhere else. No longer would the ubiquitous nine foot high fluorescent lit ceiling serve as a constant reminder of our diminished sensibilities but rather a dimensional variation in plan and section would reflect the rich array of places, both communal and private that reflect

characteristics of a village or a grand hotel. One such place is the double-height communal space which is the heart of the community at the Cardinal Ambrozic Houses of Providence long term care facility.

The notion of the house is perhaps more applicable to the resident's room—his or her house within the village, or suite within the grand hotel. Domestic attributes such as porch, means of identity, front door and view from a window combine with the capacity of the room to be personalised—large window sills, ledges, picture rails and other opportunities for the display of objects and possessions—to sustain the image of house within the larger community.

The garden is an environment that is not driven by programme or use (the antithesis of the hospital) but rather exists simply as a place of delight and joy. Here the focus shifts from an internalised world to the outdoors—sheltered and defined but with light and air as well as a reference for orientation. Raised garden beds, water features, continuous perambulating paths and shade provided by trellises and trees are common elements of the garden environment.

The house, the grand hotel, the village and the garden are paradigms which provide us with the social and cultural energy to balance the imperatives of the functional, technical and safety issues which must be satisfied. They make it possible, even in a heavy care setting, to establish a socially coherent yet varied context in which residents or patients requiring a range of special services can make their home.

holland bloorview kids
rehabilitation hospital
2006

BELOW Isometric drawing highlighting the
ground-level interior and exterior public space
from the street through to the ravine with the
transparent bridge above linking the two major
building volumes.

OPPOSITE The Hospital and entry court at night.

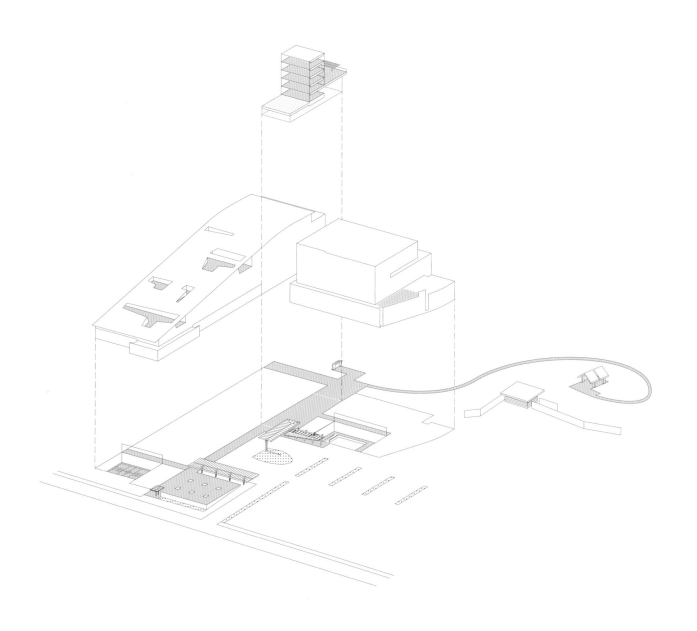

1. main entrance
2. school entrance
3. service/receiving
4. future expansion

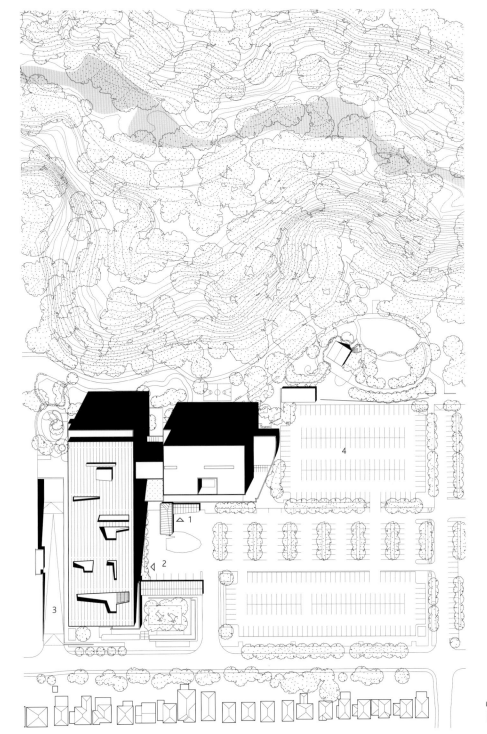

LEFT **Site plan.**

OPPOSITE LEFT **The Resource Centre,** a living room where children and their families can become familiar with the facility and its programmes while enjoying views to the ravine.

OPPOSITE RIGHT **View from entrance lobby.**

0   10   25   50m

Holland Bloorview Kids Rehabilitation Hospital is the designated Provincial resource (Province of Ontario) for rehabilitation and complex continuing care for children, young adults and their families. It is innovative in its mandate to combine all aspects of rehabilitation—research, therapy and education—in one facility. Holland Bloorview is Canada's first teaching hospital in children's rehabilitation and is home to the field's top scientists who are accommodated in research laboratories and engineering workshops.

The client's goal was to create an inspirational setting that reflects what is best for children, young adults and their families; to create a setting which speaks to a child's right to fully participate in our society.

Situated in an established residential neighbourhood at the edge of Toronto's Burke's Brook Ravine, this six-storey, 3,326 m^2 L-shaped building is a highly specialised, multi-use facility providing a wide range of services for children and young adults with disabilities. The hospital includes 75 inpatient beds, a rehabilitation centre, research laboratories and workshops, an elementary school and a recreation complex which includes a gymnasium and therapeutic pool. The school and recreation complex serve not only patients but also the neighbouring community.

OPPOSITE TOP An interior corridor becomes a gallery with places to sit overlooking the therapeutic pool.

OPPOSITE BOTTOM Two young swimmers.

RIGHT The pool material palette includes wood, concrete and a blue mosaic tile on the south wall.

OPPOSITE Out buildings with the ravine beyond.

LEFT The canopy for school bus drop off.

RIGHT The third floor exterior terrace.

The architectural vision is one of warmth, community and welcoming for the people it serves, building upon a shared belief in the benefits that a well designed healing environment can provide. The art installations and non-institutional architectural language work to firmly ground the programme elements in the unique ravine setting as well as the neighbouring residential community.

The building's sloped roof form is incised with wood-lined landscaped terraces for outdoor access and views creating a giant hillside, which unlike the adjacent ravine, is entirely accessible to children with disabilities.

The entry court is large enough to accommodate the variety of vehicles that bring children to the centre, yet there is ample shade and greenery to make it a welcoming place. The entry court operates as a threshold, mediating between the city and ravine edge where therapeutic gardens are located, offering children opportunities for play, discovery and rehabilitation.

The facility provides a hierarchy of spaces from public to private. Public spaces are open and accessible to all. Full of light and activity, these spaces encourage a connection to the ravine site and community beyond. The Resource Centre, for example, is a living room where children and their families can become familiar with the facility and its programmes while enjoying views to the ravine. More private spaces such as patient and family accommodation are infused with natural light while providing comfortable spaces that are personal and more intimate in scale.

OPPOSITE The building's sloped roof is incised
with wood-lined landscaped terraces for
outdoor access and views.

LEFT The art studio adjacent to the outdoor
art programme area on the ravine.

RIGHT The entry court looking towards the
main entry and the glass bridge connecting
the two major building volumes.

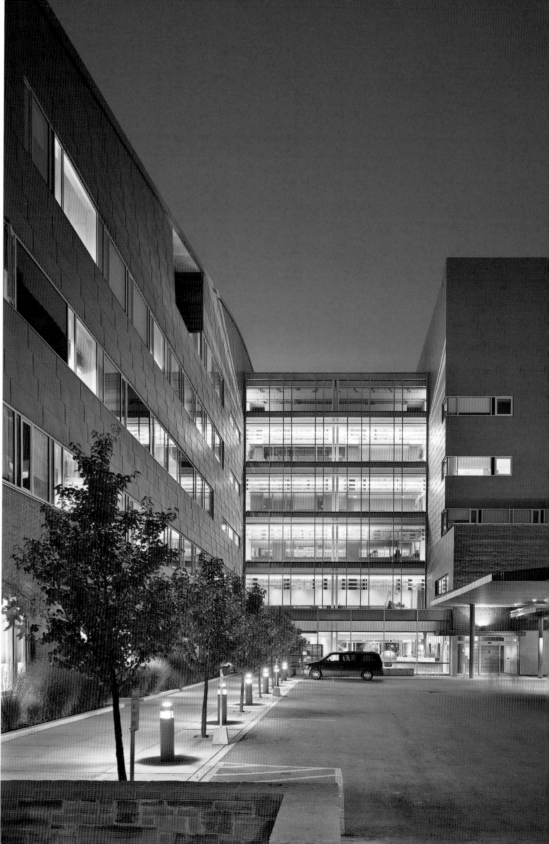

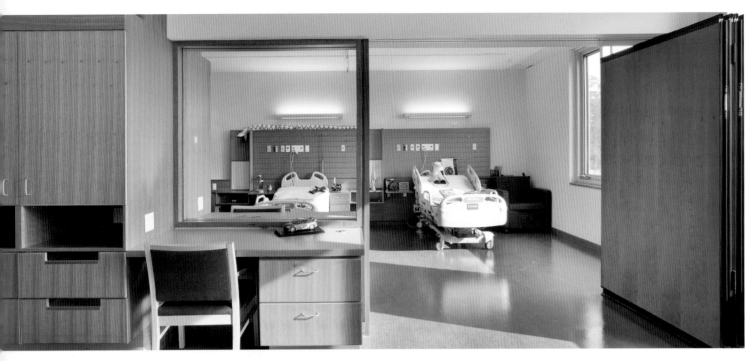

TOP **Inpatient bedroom.**

BOTTOM **The glass bridge with art installation.**

OPPOSITE **Cafeteria with views to the childrens' playground and ravine.**

Unique to this facility are 20 special art installations created by local artists and children. The artworks weave a story about the site, nature, community and history. The installations celebrate destinations and provide landmarks within the building to encourage journeying and discovery by patients and visitors through tactile and visual stimulation.

The materials reinforce the non-institutional message; zinc walls wrap from outside to inside through glass planes to break down the hard boundary between inside and outside. Limestone, wood, brick, glass and ceramic tile are complemented by a subtle palette of coloured linoleum. The emphasis on the visual and tactile grew out of an understanding that many children counterbalance their mobility limitations with compensating senses.

This project was completed as a joint venture between Montgomery Sisam Architects and Stantec Architecture.

TORONTO BOTANICAL GARDEN

OPPOSITE The pavilion at night.

BELOW Isometric drawing highlighting the green-roofed pavilion and the linear skylight between the existing structure and the new addition.

the george and kathy dembroski centre for horticulture at the toronto botanical garden
2005

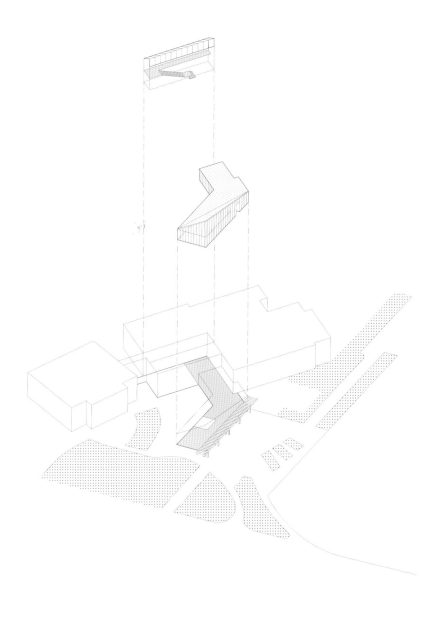

The Toronto Botanical Garden (TBG) is a charitable organisation whose purpose is to inspire passion, respect and understanding of gardening, horticulture, the natural landscape and a healthy environment.

Located in Edwards Gardens in Toronto the organisation offers educational programmes, garden tours, meeting places and an extensive horticultural library for public use. The George and Kathy Dembroski Centre for Horticulture was created at the same time as the expanded botanical gardens themselves.

The new Centre for Horticulture expands on two existing linked buildings (formerly The Civic Garden Centre) designed by architects Raymond Moriyama, 1964, and Jerome Markson, 1976. The expansion and renovation project includes an expanded library, new administrative offices, store, a children's centre and upgraded meeting rooms.

The 360 m² addition and renovation eliminated the internal and external ramps providing access to the original building, bringing all the major public functions to the ground floor level and making them universally accessible. The new addition presents itself as a park pavilion and is positioned to create two garden courts directly related to interior public spaces, effectively bringing the gardens closer to the activities inside the building.

This new fritted glass pavilion is designed as a sculpted form, mute and calm during the day and taking on the more dramatic appearance of a large lantern in the evening. Although the pavilion creates a new 'front door' to the facility, it remains deferential

OPPOSITE The pavilion sitting in front of the original Raymond Moriyama building, 1964, on the left, and the Jerome Markson addition, 1976, on the right.

TOP The fritted glass pavilion.

BOTTOM The pavilion is deferential to the gardens, providing an enclosure and tipping its green roof making it visible from this garden court.

to the gardens, providing an enclosure and tipping its green roof making it visible from one of the garden courts. A wood trellis with planting across the south-facing entry facade provides sun protection to the clear glass along the lower part of the pavilion.

Part of the existing steel structure was kept to support a new linear skylight bringing an abundance of natural light to the stair and corridor between the existing structure and the new addition. The overall design intent of the project was integration; new building with existing buildings, buildings with gardens and finally an integrated approach to issues of sustainability and green design.

In keeping with the TGB's mission of advocating stewardship of the natural environment, the additions and alterations incorporated a number of sustainable design measures including the reuse of material from the existing building and the use of stormwater held in cisterns to irrigate the extensive gardens. The Centre for Horticulture achieved a LEED® Silver rating and received the Green Toronto Award in 2006.

BELOW **Retail space in the pavilion with fritted glass above and clear glass at ground-level to allow for views out to the gardens.**

OPPOSITE **Site plan.**

1. new addition
2. existing building
   (1964)
3. existing building
   (1976)
4. garden courts
5. arrival court
6. edwards gardens

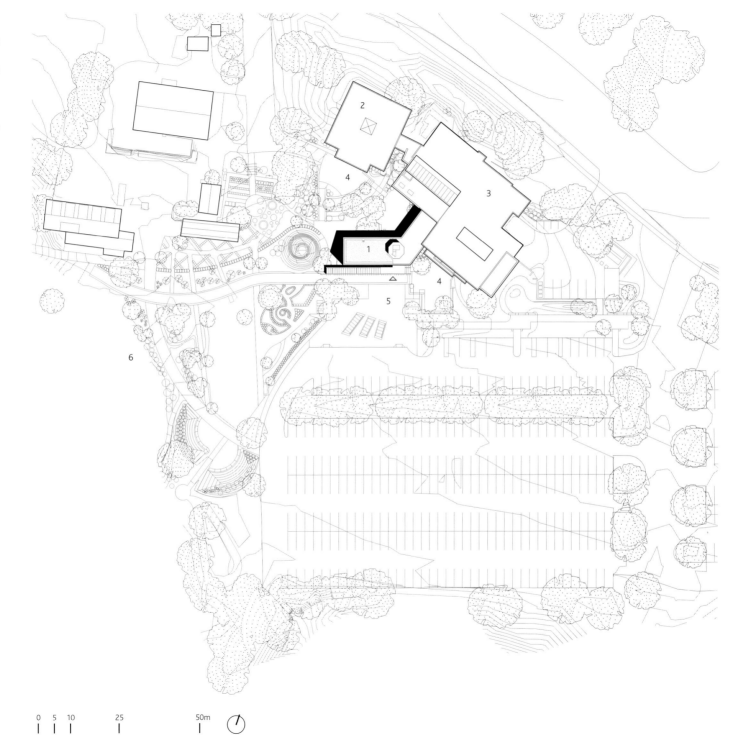

0 5 10   25   50m

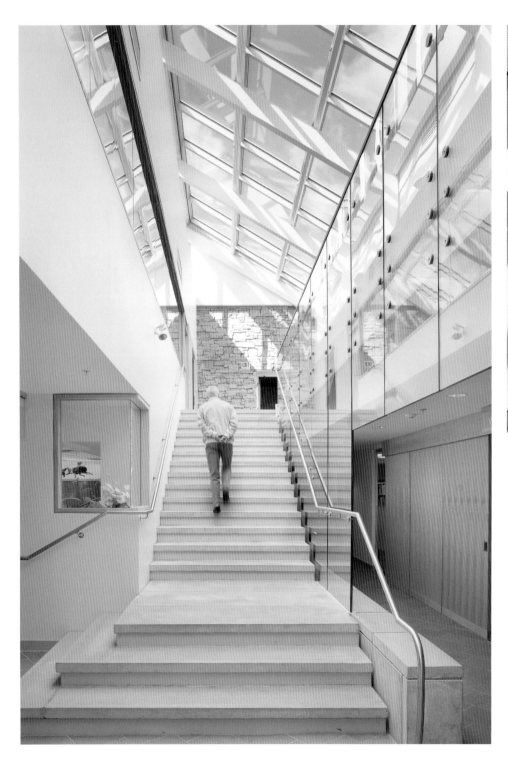

OPPOSITE Low in scale with its large sheltering roofs, the building reflects the modest agricultural structures of the area while maintaining a residential character.

BELOW Isometric drawing highlighting the major public spaces of the home with their expressive roof forms.

norview lodge long term care facility
2005

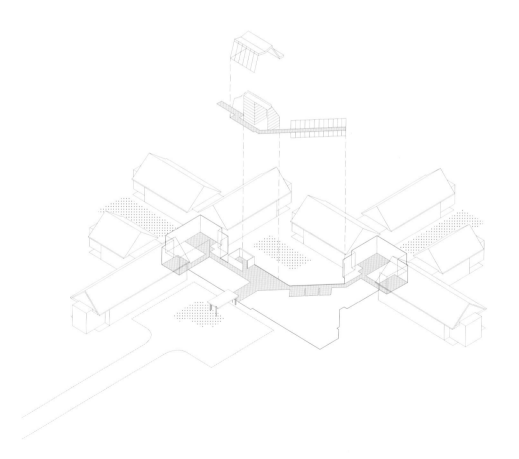

LEFT The large volume of the great room featuring its extensive use of wood and stone.

RIGHT The resident house dining area with views out to the forest.

OPPOSITE Site plan.

1. main entrance
2. great room
3. house
4. secure garden

0   10   25   50m

ABOVE **The central double-height space with its large north-facing window.**

OPPOSITE LEFT **The south exterior wall of the central building expressing the volume of the double-height space.**

OPPOSITE RIGHT **Corner windows in the resident wings.**

Norview Lodge accommodates 179 residents in two, two-storey wings of this 12,750 m² long term care facility near Simcoe, Ontario. Each wing is divided into four 'houses' for 22 to 23 residents, complete with their own living, dining, bathing and other support spaces. The more public areas of each house are accommodated at the house entrance while the resident rooms are located in a more private setting. Community amenities, including the chapel, shops, a great room and an auditorium, are grouped within a central double-height volume with high windows that face towards the entrance to the site. When lit at night, the high volume creates a welcoming beacon and strong visual presence from the road. This double-height volume features the extensive use of wood and stone to provide warmth and comfort.

Set on a cultivated site at the edge of a natural Carolinian forest, the building's wood structure and cladding allow it to fit easily into its rustic setting. The design of the building draws on the vernacular architecture of the surrounding farming community. Low in scale with large sheltering roofs, the building reflects the modest, agricultural structures of the area while maintaining a residential nature. The characteristics

of house, garden and community are the foundations of the design, reflecting a residential as opposed to institutional approach to both plan organisation and architectural expression.

Recognising that many of the residents would have been farmers who have spent much of their lives outdoors, the design establishes strong, inside and outside connections through glazed courtyards, deep porches at the end of each corridor and shaded terraces on the second floor. Large expanses of windows provide a variety of views of the surrounding landscape.

OPPOSITE The new headquarters building and the original farmhouse with the wetland marsh in the foreground.

BELOW Isometric drawing highlighting the glazed link joining the two elemental buildings and the contrasting horizontal pine screens for the stair tower and mechanical equipment.

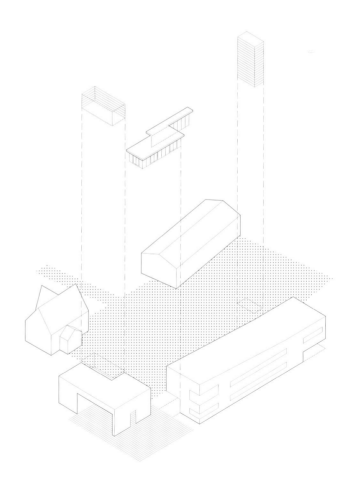

The Bird Studies Canada Headquarters provides a new office, research and educational facility for Bird Studies Canada, Canada's leading non-profit conservation organisation dedicated to advancing understanding, appreciation and conservation of wild birds and their habitats. The scope of their work is international, with exchanges and training for ornithologists, biologists and other researchers from across the hemisphere, reflecting the range of habitats that 'Canadian' wild birds depend on.

As well as consolidating its existing research and administrative facilities, the headquarters also serves as an interpretive and educational centre for the public. The programme stipulated flexible workspaces for researchers and administrators, a library to house a national wild bird database, as well as meeting rooms and a lecture hall. In addition to these requirements interior and exterior spaces are provided to assemble research teams and birding enthusiasts for field observations.

The site is a former farm overlooking the inner bay of Long Point peninsula on Lake Erie, Ontario. Designated as a World Biosphere Reserve, the peninsula is a 32 kilometre spit of sand, open fields and marshes and provides habitat for millions of water fowl and migrant land birds, with views over the expanse of Lake Erie to the south and the rolling flatlands of tobacco farms to the north.

The design of the new headquarters takes into account the existing farm buildings on the site.

BELOW Site plan.

OPPOSITE The glazed link connecting the two building volumes. The link functions as an entry to the Headquarters as well as a gateway to a large cedar viewing platform.

1. existing farm buildings
2. original farmyard
3. new building
4. wetland marsh

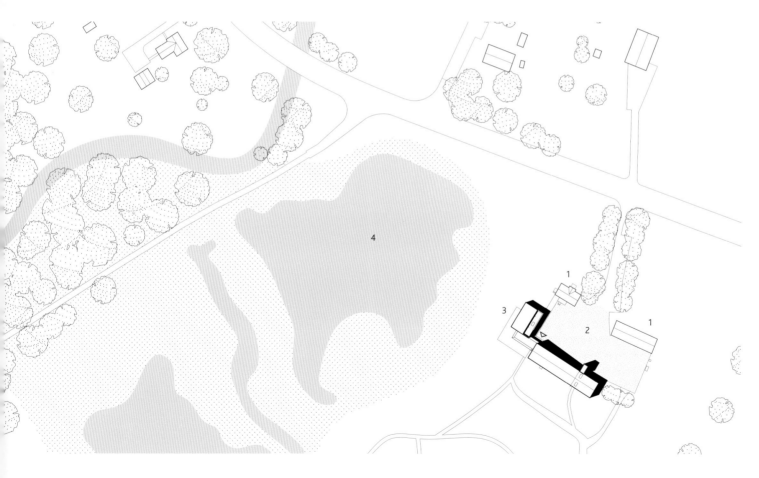

0 10 25 50m

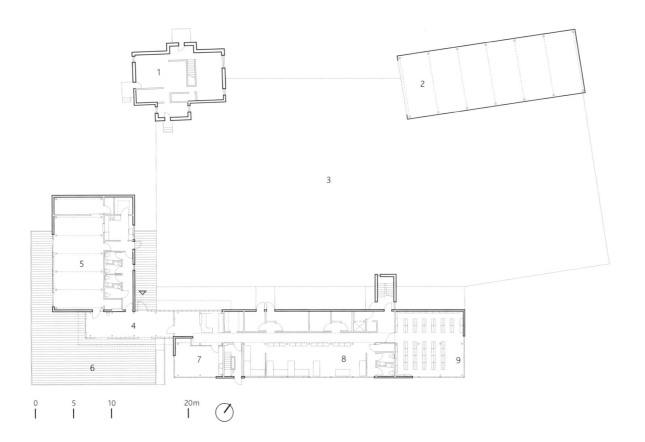

1. caretaker
2. storage
3. original farmyard
4. entrance lobby
5. lecture hall
6. viewing platform
7. conference room
8. work space
9. library

0   5   10   20m

The farm, dating back to 1797, was one of the first to be settled on the north shore of Lake Erie. The new building is organised around the original farmyard, creating a contained, informal court which serves as a multi-use arrival and service space as well as a large gathering area for special summer events.

The headquarters consists of elemental buildings. The events building takes the form of a simple cube accommodating the lecture hall and kitchen. The second building, with its gently sloping butterfly roof, functions as an office loft and includes a library and meeting rooms. Connecting these two volumes is a glazed link that functions as an entry to the headquarters as well as a gateway to a large cedar viewing platform looking out to the extensive property and adjacent wetland while framing a view to Long Point. A stair

tower projecting from the loft wing acts as a light source for the courtyard at night.

The two wood buildings are clad in dark stained cedar siding punctuated by ribbon windows framed in anodised aluminium. In contrast, the stair tower and screens for the mechanical units are clad in light stained horizontal pine.

OPPOSITE **Ground floor plan.**

LEFT **The office loft under the gently sloping butterfly roof.**

RIGHT **The cedar viewing platform.**

the cardinal ambrozic houses
of providence
2000

BELOW Isometric drawing highlighting the public areas of the building.

OPPOSITE The north entry court is developed as a landscaped piazza with low garden walls, sitting areas, planters and arbours.

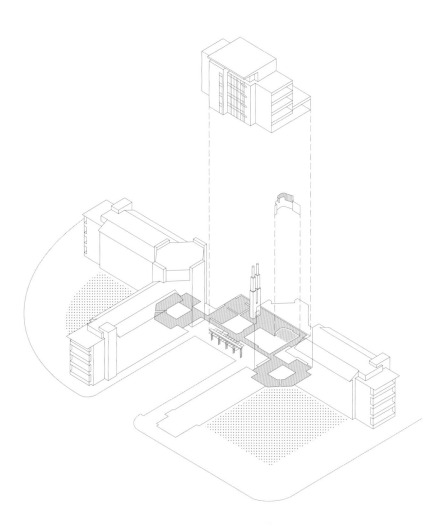

The House of Providence was founded by the Sisters of St Joseph in 1857. The institution has evolved into Providence Healthcare, providing rehabilitation, complex continuing care, long term care and community outreach with a particular focus on addressing the medical, physical, spiritual and emotional needs of individuals with sensitive conditions. Providence Healthcare is located on an 8.1 hectare site adjacent to the Warden Woods Ravine in eastern Toronto. The project began with an assessment of existing facilities and led to a master plan for the complex, evoking a campus or community atmosphere. The first phase of construction consisted of a new 288 bed long term care facility, the Cardinal Ambrozic Houses of Providence.

This new 20,438 m² building accommodates 16 houses each with 18 residents. Each house provides public areas of kitchen, dining and living spaces organised around the entrance while the resident rooms and spa are located in a more private zone.

The house facades incorporate elements associated with residential architecture such as bay windows, sloped roofs and chimneys. Each of the two L-shaped wings embraces a secure landscaped garden courtyard and is configured to maximise exposure to natural light, views and fresh air. Generous garden terraces on each floor provide easy access to outdoor space for residents. The new construction harmonises with the scale and mass of the existing hospital building to the

1. entry court
2. double-height great hall
3. house
4. secure garden
5. existing hospital

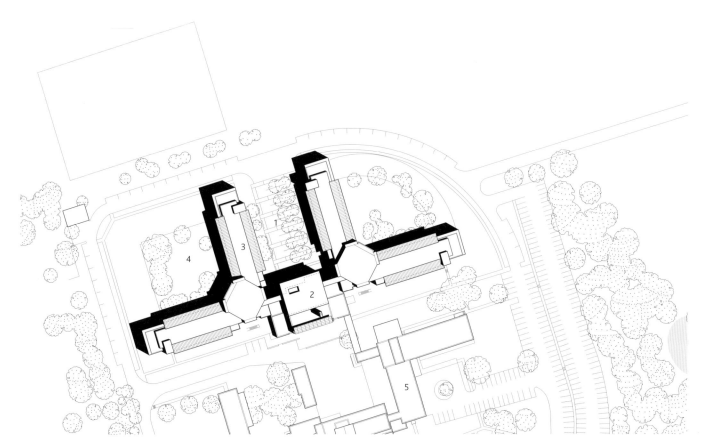

0   10   25   50m

OPPOSITE Site plan.

LEFT The front canopy.

RIGHT The main entrance.

LEFT Upper floor garden terrace with raised planting beds and wood trellises.

RIGHT Secure landscaped garden court with raised planters. The house facades incorporate elements associated with residential architecture such as bay windows, sloped roofs and chimneys.

south, and is clad in brick, precast concrete and stucco, with a sloping metal roof.

The residential wings are part of a larger community which share a variety of facilities. The heart of the community is a double-height Great Hall with a fireplace and hearth in which a range of social and recreational activities are offered. Adjacent to this space are a chapel, cafe, beauty/barbershop and general store. The north entry court is developed as a landscaped piazza with low garden walls, sitting areas, planters and arbours, creating a pleasant exterior space for residents and visitors. The garden courts and the central communal space are intended to convey a sense of generosity and scale reminiscent of the grand hotel.

This project was completed as a joint venture between Montgomery Sisam Architects and Kuwabara Payne McKenna Blumberg Architects.

LEFT **A typical bedroom with built in desk, cupboards and shelves.**

MIDDLE **A resident room entry with shelf and memory box to accommodate a favourite photograph or possession to assist the residents with dementia in recognising their own room.**

RIGHT **The double-height Great Hall with a fireplace and hearth.**

the space between

the space between

By their location and form, buildings can define an interconnected, fluid figure of open space. They are permanent and essential physical presences. Further, their combined form as an ensemble is more important than the particular formal qualities of any of them in isolation. Stefanos Polyzoides

In a period of a cult to the individual and the genius, with all due respect to genius, it is not to them that we owe our best cities. Josep Lluís Sert, 1956

Building a City

We live in an urban age. In 1910, ten per cent of the world's population lived in cities. By 2007, this had increased to 50 per cent and is projected to reach 75 per cent by the year 2050. In terms of urban models, the compact city, dense and socially diverse, brings advantages of proximity, energy efficiency and improved public health—in short, a measure of social and economic sustainability necessary to ensure our future. Density is the typical measure of the compactness of urban form and a useful metric to evaluate the viability of public transit. However, like time and space, density is a relatively abstract term without any qualitative implication. Density is the mean annual rainfall of urban metrics. Two cities that experience the same mean annual rainfall can have markedly different experiences if in one city the rain is spread equally across 365 days of the year whereas in the other city it occurs all in one week. So it is with density.

What is really going to determine the quality of the urban fabric in the compact city is the nature of the built form as well as the diversity and mixture of uses. The success of the city fabric is governed by how each act of building goes beyond the internal programme requirements of the particular structure to enhance the public realm of the city. This level of responsibility is beautifully articulated in Louis Kahn's description of a street as "a room by agreement; a community room, the walls of which belong to the donors, dedicated to the city for common use". The spaces and elements in between—

TOP A habitable private garden, ROAG house proposal.

BOTTOM University of Virginia by Thomas Jefferson.

OPPOSITE TOP Säynätsalo Town Hall by Alvar Aalto.

OPPOSITE MIDDLE Charleston single house.

OPPOSITE BOTTOM Kings Road House, Los Angeles by Rudolph Schindler.

the streets, squares, laneways, porches, colonnades, canopies are the life blood of the city and the people using those spaces who are generally not on the building committee are part of the multiple client group that must be considered through any act of building. The issue of context has always played an important generative role in the design of our projects.

We have attempted to establish reciprocity between building and site such that the integrity of the building is matched by concerns about reinforcing new or existing streets, squares or courtyards. In Don Mount Court/Rivertowne we have reclaimed a former urban street pattern and created a new urban square in rebuilding social housing that, built in the 1960s, was isolated from the surrounding neighbourhood. Market units were incorporated into this regeneration project to provide economic viability and social diversity. New homes respect and reinforce the scale and character of the surrounding neighbourhood with their porches and garden pathways. Integration into the urban fabric and diversity of built form and use was also central to our Master Plan for rebuilding the 11 hectare site for the Centre for Addiction and Mental Health in Toronto.

City building often involves generating new uses for or simply rehabilitating historic structures. The regeneration of a former book binding factory into new housing and the rehabilitation of a store on Queen Street West in Toronto are examples of such initiatives.

The space between is typically the domain of pedestrians and cyclists in addition to public transit and the already well provided for automobile. The design of iconic bridges—John Street, Humber River and Fort York is our attempt to support and enhance the realm of the pedestrian and/or the cyclist through design of enduring quality.

In the ROAG (rooms on a garden) house proposal, we tried to define a new paradigm for single family housing—a mix of single family houses and town houses to achieve a density range of 37 to 54 units per hectare. Inspired by the Charleston Single House, the houses are arranged on lots to positively define and make habitable the outdoor places—streets, lanes, gardens and patios, leaving no residual or wasted space so often found in suburban single family housing. One house forms the garden wall for the next house in a spirit of urban cooperation.

There is a congruence between urbanism, environmentalism and issues of public health that demand a more holistic, collaborative and thoughtful approach to building in the city—one that views building the city as a significant component

of making a building or other structure in the city. As Peter Calthorpe states in his book, *Urbanism in the Age of Climate Change*, "Urbanism is a climate change antibiotic—urbanism is, in fact, our single most potent weapon against climate change, rising energy costs and environmental degradation."

Establishing Place

Ultimately it is the sense of reciprocity between building and site that create places which play a dignified and lasting role for the building's occupants and the wider community. Inspirational and influential precedents for this notion of this sense of reciprocity between building and site are as varied as the Charleston Single House, Rudolph Schindler's Kings Road House in Los Angeles, Alvar Aalto's Säynätsalo Town Hall and Thomas Jefferson's University of Virginia. In these settings the outdoor places are every bit as compelling as the indoor places and they are strongly engaged with one another.

Outside of an urban context, the built form proposed must take clues from the site whether it has a building context such as a campus (a variant of the urban context) or simply a distinct topography, tree cover, orientation, set of views... all of which should inflect the built form. The building can also be configured to create exterior places, in a sense creating its own urbanity. The long porch at Glen Stor Dun Lodge is an acknowledgment of a panoramic south-facing view over the St Lawrence River. The George and Kathy Dembroski Centre for Horticulture addition to the Toronto Botanical Gardens is positioned to create a series of garden courts directly related to interior public spaces and effectively brings the gardens closer to the activities inside the building.

Some projects have a responsibility to redress and repair conditions where the existing built form has either not responded to a compelling natural site condition or has created a residual and undefined placelessness. The addition at the Granite Club will embrace an extraordinary ravine setting in ways that the existing building hadn't done while the Arts Administration Building at the University of Toronto at Scarborough takes on a significant role in repairing a degraded campus fabric. Whether it is a rural, suburban or urban context, the quality of the 'space between' contributes significantly to that setting's sense of place.

OPPOSITE A street view showing one of the three transitional inpatient care buildings on the left and office space housing the Addiction Outpatient programmes on the right.

BELOW Isometric drawings illustrating the project's phasing from existing (2001), present (2012), and the ultimate build out of the 'urban village' scheduled for 2020.

centre for addiction and mental health
2008, 2012

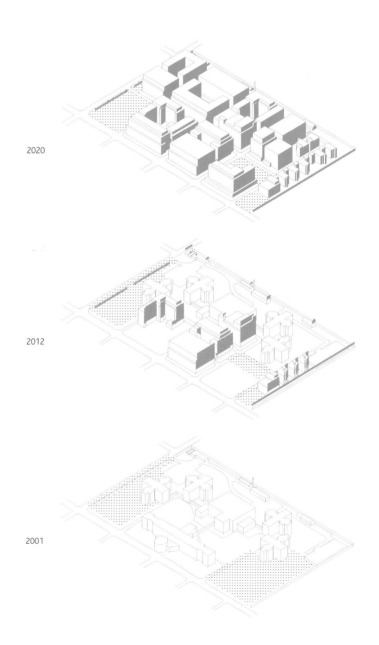

2020

2012

2001

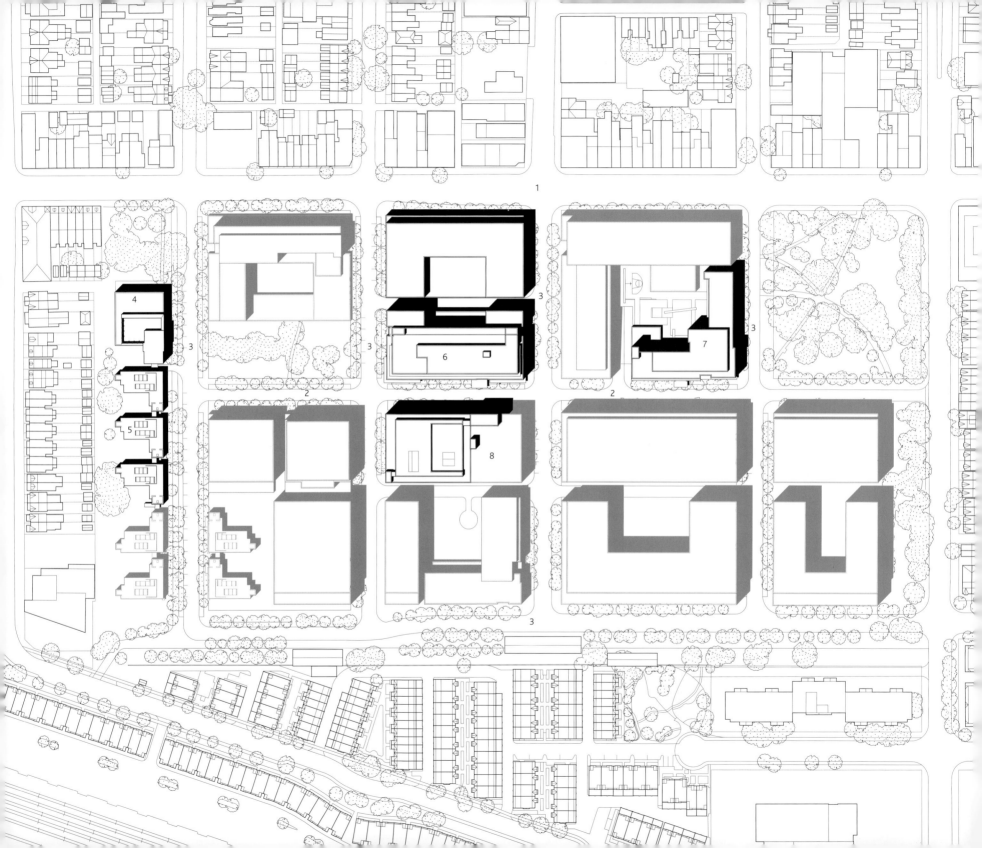

OPPOSITE **Site plan.**

LEFT **The front entrance to the Bell Gateway building, accommodating outpatient services and central administration.**

RIGHT **A new street in the 'urban village'.**

1. queen street west
2. stokes street (new)
3. new extensions of existing streets
4. addiction outpatient services
5. transitional client care
6. bell gateway building
7. intergenerational wellness centre
8. parking and utilities building

0   10   25   50m

The Centre for Addiction and Mental Health (CAMH), the largest mental health/addiction treatment and research facility in Canada is undergoing a major transformation on its 11 hectare site, in a mixed retail and residential urban neighbourhood in Toronto. Built originally as a Provincial Asylum in 1849, CAMH had evolved as an institutional campus of patient care and administrative buildings, interconnected with links, creating an internalised clinical and isolated environment for both clients and staff.

In combating the stigma long associated with mental disorder and addiction, CAMH developed the vision in 1998 to create an 'urban village' for its comprehensive site redevelopment. In 2001 Montgomery Sisam Architects, as part of Community Care Consortium (C3), won a design competition to develop a Master Plan with the goal of fully integrating mental healthcare into the community in order to provide a more normalised treatment environment for clients. By extending the existing fabric of city streets surrounding the site, the hospital's new buildings are and will be distributed on different city blocks amongst other mixed-use non-hospital buildings, in order to contribute to the revitalisation of both the centre and the neighbourhood. The Centre's diverse programme includes multi-use academic spaces, research facilities and client treatment and care complexes within an urban setting.

The first phase of this redevelopment is a pilot project designed for 72 clients in the Addiction and Mood and Anxiety programmes. The concept of 'urban integration' is supported by the construction of three distinct apartment-like buildings, each accommodating

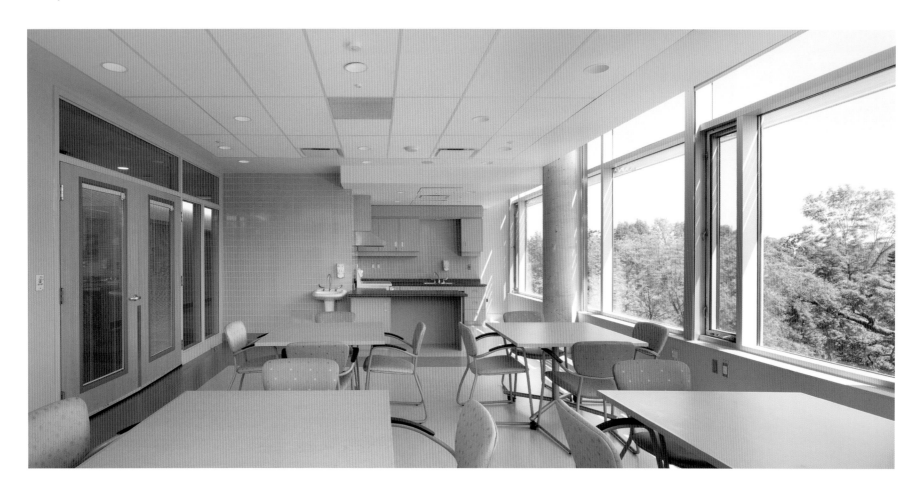

24 clients along a tree-lined city street. A separate flexible, generic office building houses the Addiction Outpatient programmes.

The key to the success of this new facility is the creation of a home-like environment that is filled with ample natural light and views to the outdoors. An intimate social milieu is created by the grouping of six clients on each of the four floors. Each client has a private bedroom and WC, and shares the use of living/dining and kitchen. Each building has a large landscaped courtyard garden to which all clients have easy physical and visual access. The entry and

lounges for each building have a direct relation to the courtyards. The courtyard provides therapeutic use as well as opportunities for informal social gathering and interaction between clients and staff members. This house and garden setting reinforces the vision of a normalising, healing environment that fosters and supports clients' recovery and return to the community.

The second phase of the redevelopment consists of two new significant buildings, which contribute to the urban fabric of the community while exemplifying a more integrated approach to normalising the healing environment. The Intergenerational Wellness

ABOVE **The dining room with views and abundant natural light on an adolescent inpatient unit of the Intergenerational Wellness Centre.**

OPPOSITE LEFT **Each of the three transitional client care buildings has a large landscaped courtyard garden to which all clients have easy physical and visual access. The original wall of the old asylum provides a backdrop for the courts.**

OPPOSITE RIGHT **A corner window with window seat in the apartment lounge looking out over the city.**

Centre, an acute inpatient facility, accommodates outpatient services for children and adolescents as well as inpatient care for geriatric and adolescent clients, reflecting the current needs in our diverse society. The Bell Gateway Building combines multiple outpatient services and the hospital's central administrative functions, again breaking down the segregation between the institution and the clients that it serves.

Transitional Client Care Buildings were completed by a joint venture consortium C3 (Kuwabara Payne McKenna Blumberg Architects, Montgomery Sisam Architects and Kearns Mancini Architects).

For the Intergenerational Wellness Centre, Bell Gateway Building and Parking and Utilities Building the joint venture consortium C3 (Kuwabara Payne McKenna Blumberg Architects, Montgomery Sisam Architects and Kearns Mancini Architects) were responsible for the design exemplar. C3 + Cannon Design were the Planning, Design and Compliance Architects, responsible for the Project Specific Output Specifications.

Stantec Architects were the architects for the Design, Build, Finance and Maintain consortium responsible for the design through construction. They are the Architects of Record.

LEFT **A bedroom in the Transitional Client Care Building.**

RIGHT **A view to the Transitional Client Care Building and office space from the north side of Queen Street.**

OPPOSITE **A street view of the Transitional Client Care Building. The solid masonry stair tower contrasts with the transparent bridge with views through to the garden court while communal dining and lounge spaces have a different expression than the punched windows of the bedrooms.**

OPPOSITE Street life on the new Munroe Street. A simple robust building vocabulary was developed, picking up on the scale, proportion and material of the existing neighbourhood.

BELOW Isometric drawings illustrating the original (1968) Don Mount Court comprising 232 low income rental units on the bottom and the replacement scheme (232 low income rental units and 187 marked ownership units) on the top.

don mount court/rivertowne
2011

2011

1968

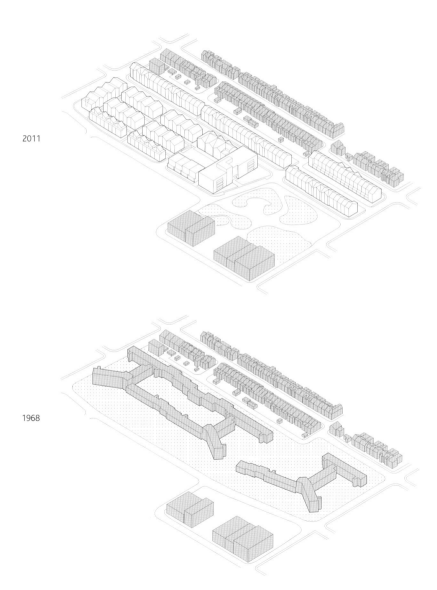

BELOW **Garden pathways serving the three-
-and-a-half-storey grade related stacked
townhouses.**

OPPOSITE **Site plan.**

The original Don Mount Court, 1968, provided new housing for low income households. The design, typical for its time, replaced city streets and houses with four- and six-storey buildings set in a self-contained property with the ground plane largely taken up by parking and residual open space. The unintended consequence of this approach resulted in a 'project' isolated from the surrounding community.

In 2000, an engineering study revealed that there was extensive deterioration of the concrete structure of the original buildings. The Toronto Community Housing Corporation, based on the engineering study as well as tenant and community input, decided to recreate Don Mount Court as a mixed-income community, rebuilding the 232 low income rental units and integrating them with new market ownership housing. The rental units are rebuilt as stacked townhouses and a fully accessible low-rise apartment building accommodating a wide range of unit types ranging from studio apartments to five-bedroom family units. The 187 market ownership units are organised in stacked townhouses over a single level underground parking garage. The stacked townhouses are a maximum of three-and-a-half-storeys and all have grade related access either on the street or on garden pathways.

The regeneration of Don Mount Court (renamed Rivertowne) relies on the integration of the new

1. dundas street
2. munroe street
3. carroll street
4. four-storey apartment building
5. new urban square
6. existing industrial buildings
7. don river valley

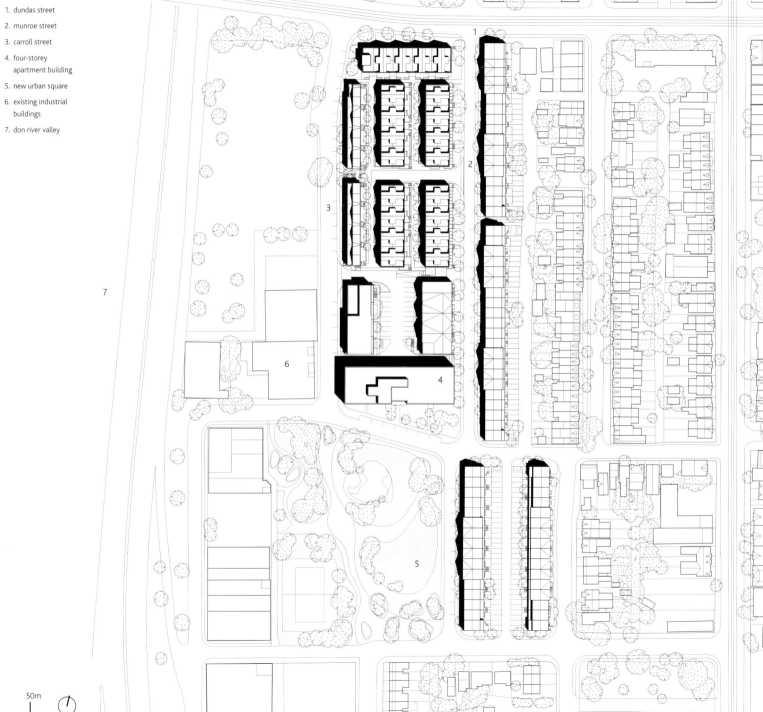

0 10 25   50m

LEFT The flat roofed apartment building
in the background reflects the language of
the existing brick industrial building in the
foreground.

RIGHT Integration is achieved through an
archetypal Toronto pattern of streets and
laneways that connect with the existing
urban fabric. Shown here is the extension of
Munroe Street into the new housing.

OPPOSITE The roofscape of the new
development as seen from across the
Don River Valley.

mixed income community with the surrounding neighbourhood. Integration is achieved through an archetypal Toronto pattern of urban square, streets and laneways that connect with the existing urban fabric. A new square is created by consolidating the formerly dispersed open spaces while existing city streets are extended into the new community.

The surrounding neighbourhood is made up of largely individual or semi-detached Victorian houses. Since it was not possible (or necessarily desirable) to replicate the detailing of these houses within a restricted budget, a simpler more robust vocabulary was developed, picking up on the scale, proportion and material of the existing neighbourhood. Components of this vocabulary (gables, bay window, canopies…) are incorporated in a variety of ways, creating sufficient complexity to break down the sense of this being one large project. While the townhouses respect and reinforce the physical characteristics of the nearby housing fabric, the flat roofed apartment building on the square reflects the language of the brick industrial buildings to the south and west.

This project was completed as a joint venture between Montgomery Sisam Architects and Kearns Mancini Architects.

OPPOSITE The classical main entrance portico of the renovated industrial building on Carlaw Avenue.

BELOW Isometric drawing highlighting the building components including the renovated three-storey industrial building, the new stacked townhouses on Boston Avenue and the new eight-storey glass tower.

printing factory lofts
2009

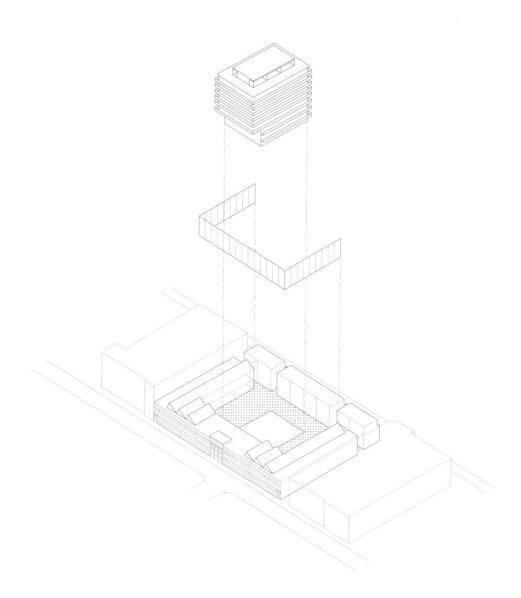

Originally built to house the printing presses of Rolph-Clark-Stone, a Toronto-based lithographic and fine printing company, 201 Carlaw Avenue has been a Leslieville landmark since its completion in 1913 when this community was at the heart of industry in Toronto. The client's objectives for the site were twofold: first, to design housing that would appeal to the sophisticated Toronto market and second, to reinvigorate and repurpose a local landmark and significant piece of the city's heritage. The repurposing of this abandoned industrial building has introduced 254 new housing units into this evolving neighbourhood in response to the growing demand for housing in the city.

The Printing Factory Lofts preserve a portion of the three-storey factory building, a U-shaped configuration bordering the north, west and south lot lines. A new eight-storey glass tower addition is inserted in the centre of the site creating two garden courts while new stacked townhouses are placed along Boston Avenue, the residential street bordering the east edge of the site. The preserved portion of the factory has been fully converted into residential loft suites integrating the original form of the 'sawtooth' industrial skylights. The Carlaw Avenue facade has been restored and the classical main entrance portico opens to a grand wooden staircase below a coffered ceiling.

BELOW **The view along Carlaw Avenue.**

OPPOSITE LEFT **Diagrams showing, from top to bottom, the carving out and rebuilding of the site to accommodate housing around two garden courts.**

OPPOSITE RIGHT **Site plan.**

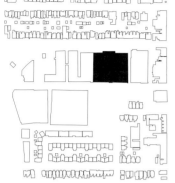

1. carlaw avenue
2. boston avenue
3. main entrance
4. garden courts

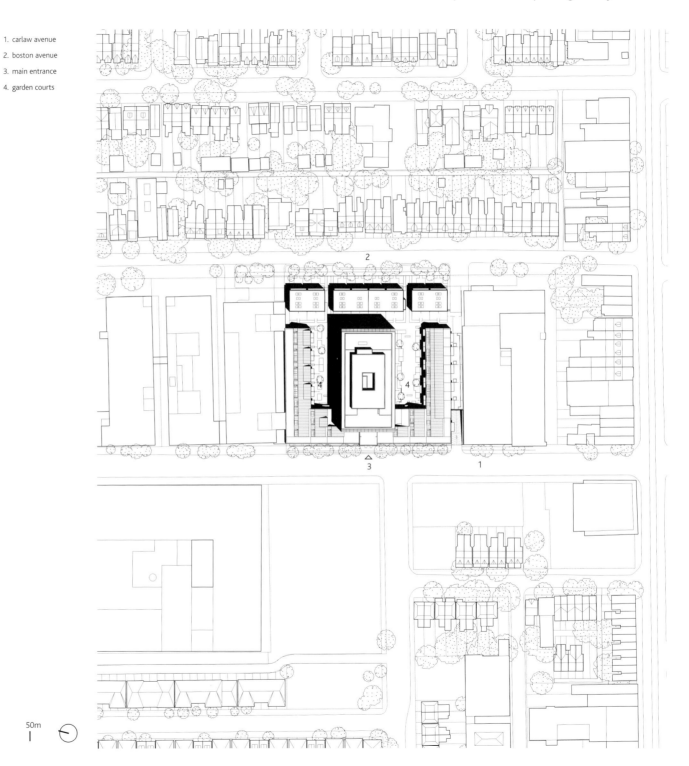

0 10 25   50m

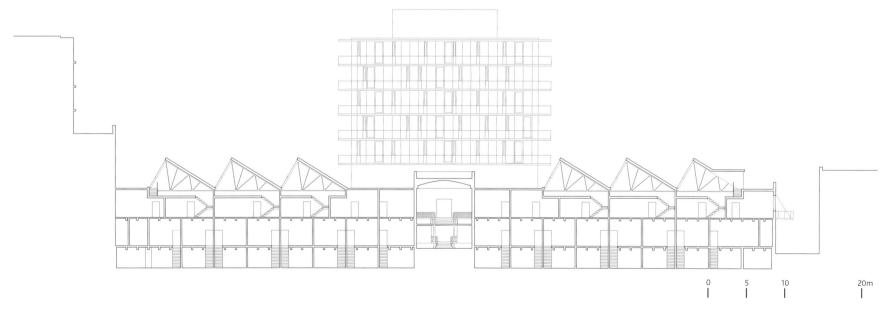

0   5   10   20m

OPPOSITE TOP LEFT **The glass balconies on the eight-storey tower.**

OPPOSITE TOP RIGHT **Garden court in winter.**

OPPOSITE BOTTOM **Section showing the preserved portion of the factory integrating the original form of the 'sawtooth' industrial skylights and the central grand staircase.**

ABOVE **Townhouses along Boston Avenue. An unused rail spur was reclaimed, creating a wide expanse of green in front of the townhouses.**

The garden courts, private yards and street frontages were designed to integrate the industrial podium into the surrounding neighbourhood while accommodating two levels of parking underground. Along Boston Avenue, an unused rail spur has been reclaimed, creating a wide expanse of green in front of the townhouses.

The project contributes to the diversity and dynamism of the surrounding Leslieville area by offering one-, two- and three-bedroom units in the tower, live/work studio units in the original building and family-sized townhouses along Boston Avenue. It also provides appropriately scaled frontages on Carlaw Avenue and Boston Avenue while at the same time creating light-filled and eminently useable garden courts within the complex.

This project was completed as a joint venture between Montgomery Sisam Architects and Chandler Graham Architects.

OPPOSITE A view of the bridge from the Humber River looking out to Lake Ontario.

BELOW Isometric drawing highlighting the structural components. Loads from the bridge deck are supported by tapered steel beams which run perpendicular to the deck. The beams are, in turn, supported by stainless steel rods that are suspended from the large steel arches that span from one side of the river to the other, anchored by the cairn-like concrete abutments.

the humber river bicycle and pedestrian bridge
1996

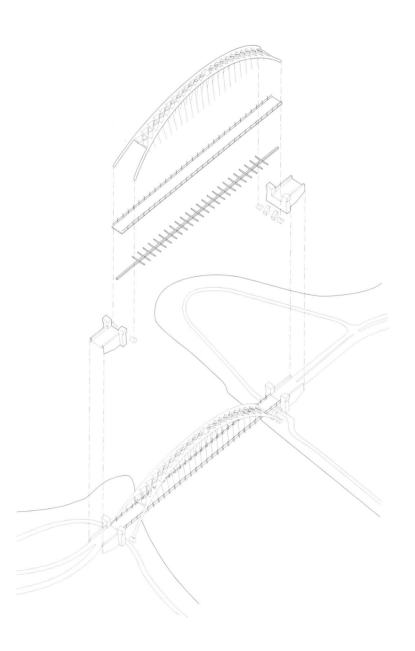

LEFT Site plan.

OPPOSITE **Stainless steel rods supporting the beams and bridge deck.**

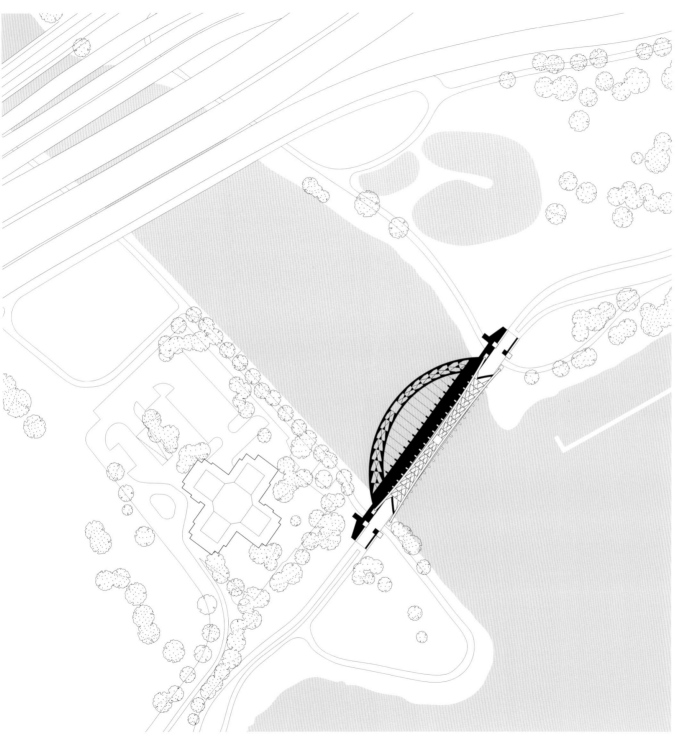

0 10 25 50m

The Humber River Bicycle and Pedestrian Bridge was one component of a large urban transportation project that involved the complete reconstruction of the aging vehicular bridges crossing the Humber River in Toronto. The idea for a separate bicycle pedestrian bridge was developed through an open planning process and a community-wide desire for a high level of public access along the waterfront. The 140 metre long Humber Bridge forms part of the Martin Goodman Waterfront Trail which extends for 56 kilometres along Toronto's waterfront.

The bridge deals with the structural forces in a simple and elegant manner. Loads from the bridge deck are supported by tapered steel beams which run perpendicular to the deck. The beams are, in turn, supported by stainless steel rods which are suspended from the large steel arches that span from one side of the river to the other.

Incorporated into the mandate for this project was a desire to recognise both the social and natural history of the site and reflect that history in the physical structures. The arch form of the bridge and the cairn-like concrete abutments on either side of the river mark a gateway to what was once the historic aboriginal trading route from Lake Ontario to Lake Simcoe and Georgian Bay to the north. The totemic head-like form of the abutments are reminiscent in scale and material to the monuments associated with the Queen Elizabeth Way, a highway which in its original form started westward from the Humber River.

Aboriginal motifs and references to the social and natural history of the site enrich the project

throughout. The steel superstructure connecting the two tubular arches is patterned as an abstract image of the Thunderbird—ruler of all airborne species—an icon (itself an abstract image) of the Woodland native peoples who frequented the site for more than 200 years. Etched panels depicting the complex and varied history of the site are located on walkways beneath the bridge deck. Snake and turtle motifs were incorporated in recognition of the natural world which once inhabited and, with proper management, will re-inhabit the mouth of the Humber River.

Since its construction, the bridge has become a popular local landmark and a destination for photography, filmmaking and various events.

The bridge was designed in association with Delcan Corporation, Bridge Engineers.

OPPOSITE The bridge from below.

RIGHT The steel superstructure connecting the two tubular arches is patterned as an abstract image of the Thunderbird—ruler of all airborne species—an icon (itself an abstract image) of the Woodland native peoples who frequented the site for more than 200 years.

OPPOSITE The prow which faces the main entrance drive has a large two-storey window marking a clear entry point to the campus as a whole and the Welcome Centre in particular.

BELOW Isometric drawing highlighting the building's strategic positioning to both extend the crescent form of the existing Science Wing and to create new routes and a series of landscaped courts including a second floor green roof.

the arts and administration building
university of toronto at scarborough
2005

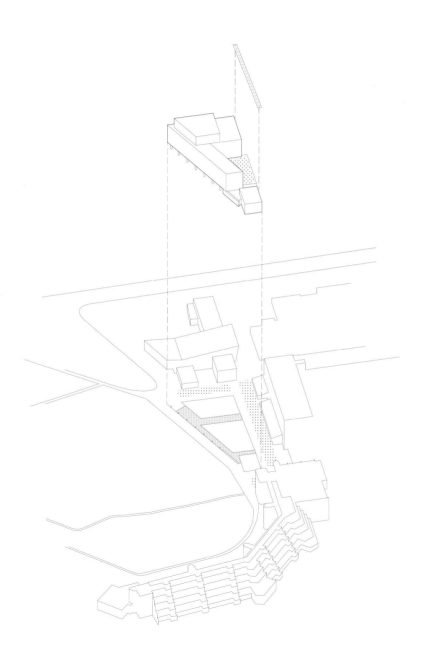

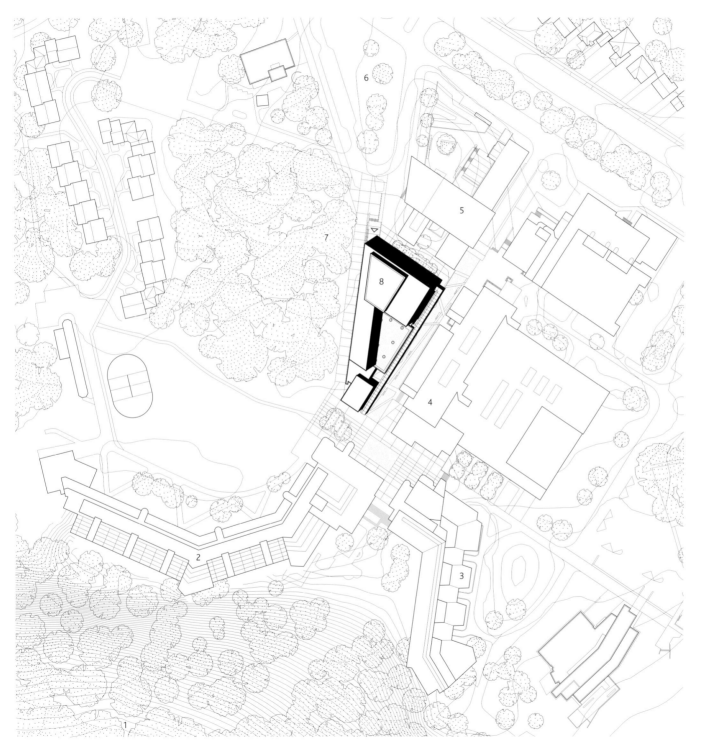

1. highland creek ravine
2. science wing
3. humanities wing
4. bladen building
5. student centre
6. main entrance to
   campus
7. woodlot
8. arts and
   administration building

0 10   25   50m

OPPOSITE Site plan.

RIGHT Secondary entrance at the north side
of the Council Chamber.

The Scarborough campus is one of three campuses of the University of Toronto and is located 35 kilometres from the downtown campus. The original Master Plan and the two initial buildings for the campus—the Humanities and Science Wings—were designed in the 1960s by the Toronto-based Australian architect John Andrews. The buildings received international acclaim at the time. An exemplar of New Brutalism, the design consisted of bold concrete forms terraced dramatically down the edge of Highland Creek ravine—possibly the first buildings in the city to respond to the organic ravine alignment, rather than the city's orthogonal urban grid.

This spectacular beginning was followed by a few decades of some very ordinary and architecturally undistinguished expansion on the table land. In the last ten years, however, a well considered major renewal and infill of the campus has taken place in response to a substantial increase in student enrolment. A key component in that renewal was the construction of the Arts and Administration Building.

The Arts and Administration Building is a 5,110 m² four-storey multi-purpose academic building housing classrooms, art and music studies, a 300-seat lecture theatre, academic and administrative offices, the

ABOVE **View from above to a landscaped courtyard and glass covered walkway.**

OPPOSITE **Ground floor plan.**

1. main entrance
2. glazed walkway
3. welcome centre
4. registration
5. 300-seat lecture theatre
6. lecture theatre foyer
7. council chamber
8. glass covered walkway
9. landscaped courtyards

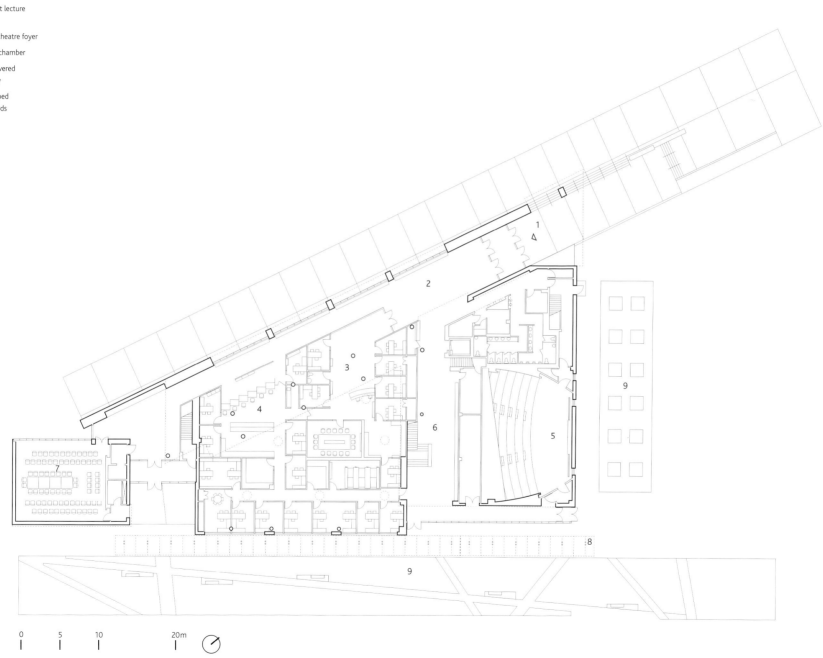

0   5   10   20m

Registrar's office, a Welcome Centre and a new Council Chamber. The new building accommodates this very complex programme but, given its key location, also takes on the role of repairing and reasserting a framework for the surrounding campus fabric. The buff brick and limestone building is positioned to extend the crescent form of the Andrews Science Wing while creating a clear entry point to the campus as a whole and the Welcome Centre in particular. The new building masks the undistinguished Bladen Building to the east, creating a series of landscaped courtyards from previously residual and undefined outdoor spaces. A glass covered exterior walkway along the east edge of the new building provides a direct connection from both the Science Wing and the Bladen Building to the new Student Centre to the north.

The north and west edges rise to four storeys with the upper three floors bordering and viewing onto a green roof over the ground floor. Skylights provide supplementary daylight to the Welcome Centre and registration areas on the ground floor below. A double-height fritted glass Council Chamber terminates the building's south end at the main east–west access route from the eastern precinct of the campus. Amply lit by natural daylight, the Council Chamber acts as a large glowing lantern at night.

BELOW **View from the glazed walkway to the woodlot beyond.**

OPPOSITE TOP **Lecture theatre foyer with stair to the second floor.**

OPPOSITE BOTTOM **Section through the 300-seat lecture theatre.**

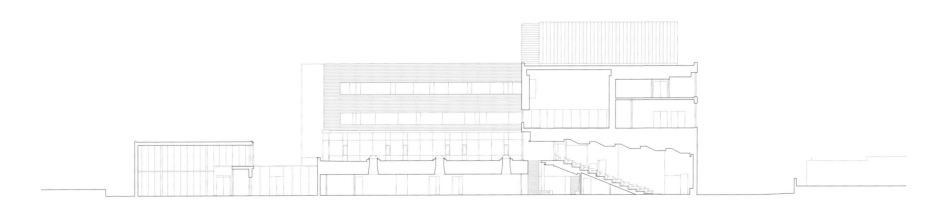

0   5   10   20m

tommy thompson park
infrastructure project
2012

BELOW Isometric drawing showing the locations of the four park pavilions on the Leslie Street Spit.

OPPOSITE View of the environmental shelter from the wetlands.

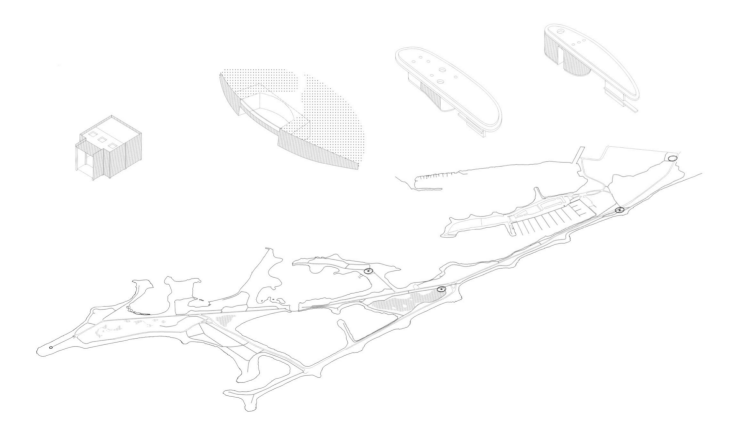

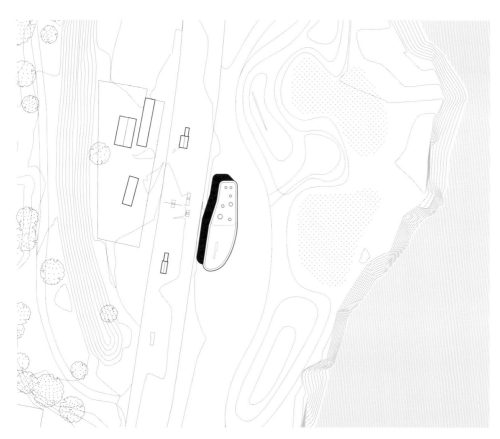

Managed by the Toronto and Region Conservation Authority (TRCA), Tommy Thompson Park is an integral part of Toronto's Lake Ontario Waterfront. The Park is located on the Leslie Street Spit, a man-made peninsula, and provides a unique urban wilderness environment in downtown Toronto that receives more than 250,000 visitors per year. Since its construction began in 1959, millions of cubic metres of concrete, earth fill, dredged sand and construction waste have built the foundation for this remarkable landscape. The site now extends about five kilometres into Lake Ontario and is 470 hectares in area. From this humble beginning, Tommy Thompson Park has developed into a complex mosaic of habitats which support a diverse selection of plants and wildlife including 56 breeding bird species.

In the context of trying to achieve a fine balance between habitat preservation and public use, the Tommy Thompson Park Infrastructure Project consists of a series of small pavilions, designed as elemental shelters with varying degrees of enclosure. They support the enjoyment, management and interpretation of the park, without disturbing its character as an urban wilderness. The structures relate to the landscape with varying degrees of integration depending on their respective uses.

The Gateway marks an entrance to the park, providing a single point of entry for vehicular, bicycle and pedestrian traffic. It includes a physical gate to the park, display space for park information, shelter, restrooms and storage.

The Staff Booth located at the narrowest section of the man-made peninsula allows TRCA staff to interact with park visitors, providing shelter from the elements

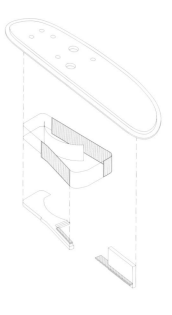

OPPOSITE TOP LEFT **Site plan of the Staff Booth.**

OPPOSITE TOP RIGHT **Staff Booth interior showing sky-lit exhibition space (nearing completion).**

OPPOSITE BOTTOM **Isometric drawing of the Staff Booth.**

TOP LEFT **Site plan of the Environmental Shelter.**

TOP RIGHT **View out from the environmental shelter.**

BOTTOM **Isometric drawing of the Environmental Shelter.**

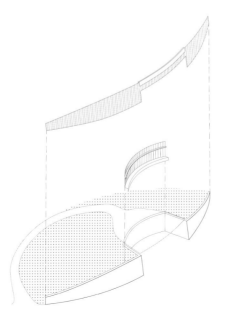

and a place to wait for the shuttle bus service. Existing surrounding berms have been re-shaped to frame views to Lake Ontario and direct pedestrian traffic to the booth while providing an informal seating area for outdoor multimedia presentations.

The Environmental Shelter is nested under a hillside on the shore of the first of a series of wetland habitats. It provides visitors with long range views from an accessible vegetated roof as well as sheltered views from a covered outdoor classroom below.

The Bird Banding and Research Station is both internally flexible and fully transportable as the best location for the mist nets used to capture birds can change from year to year.

A particular quality of the Leslie Street Spit is its ability to transform man-made material and construction waste into the foundation for a natural environment that supports a unique ecology. It is this transformational power of nature that has inspired the approach to this project, particularly in the use of materials and the manner in which the structures are conceived. The structures are designed with robust, inert materials. All the interventions are minimalist in terms of both materials and systems, designed to withstand the harsh elements with minimal maintenance.

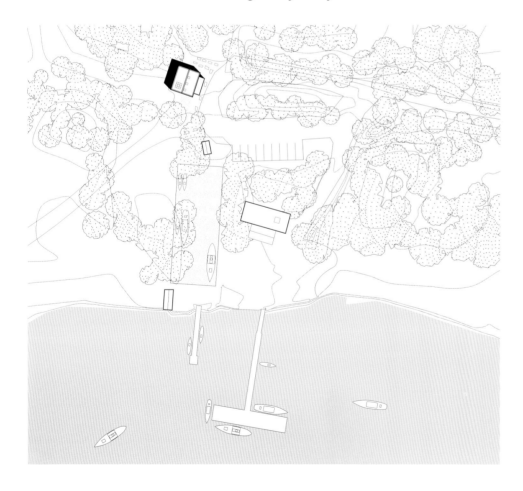

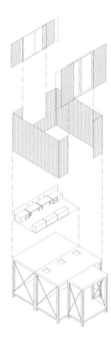

OPPOSITE LEFT Site plan showing the Bird Banding and Research Station.

OPPOSITE RIGHT Isometric of the Bird Banding and Research Station showing its various components, including the Corten steel cladding.

LEFT Bird Banding and Research Station.

RIGHT Interior of the Bird Banding and Research Station.

an architecture of generous inclusion
ken greenberg

At a time when architecture too frequently seems to be divided into high style obsessed with image making and a mundane form of practice with few ambitions and value engineered into bland conformity it is extremely encouraging to see the course charted by the work of Montgomery Sisam Architects. Their work is refreshing to see and experience—engaging, resourceful, putting users first, making us at home in our world, enhancing our daily life experiences, not showboating but elegant and cheerful. Aren't those the key roles of architecture after all? According to Vitruvius *solid useful and beautiful*.

This is a practice that from the outset and ever since has consistently focused on the needs of the vulnerable—the aged, the infirm, the sick and mobility impaired—in buildings including an impressive range of healthcare facilities and residences. In each case these architects have with great ingenuity and care sought to dignify daily life activities and routines, meeting demanding functional requirements while providing grace notes and places for sociable encounters that were not necessarily called for (or budgeted for) in the programme.

Accessibility in all senses is made a priority well beyond the requirements of the Disabilities Act for unencumbered movement. Access to daylight and greenery and the glimpses of life in the city are constant features of their repertory. By thinning the plans of residences from the earlier Belmont House to the recent Ronald McDonald House, they can be molded to shape landscaped courtyards enlivened by water, artworks, and gardens, both inward facing and open to the surrounding streets. These space-forming buildings exhibit a sophisticated urbanity providing privacy and intimacy for their inhabitants while making a valuable contribution to their neighbourhoods. Creature comforts, and sensitivity to climate and great attention to the thresholds between the inner and outer worlds are all hallmarks of the work of this firm. Their highly useable courts and gardens provide access to the outdoors both at street level and on roof terraces and balconies with shading and coverings that enhance their comfort and expand the territory available to their inhabitants.

The work of Montgomery Sisam also pays a particular attention to the in-between and often forgotten spaces inside buildings—the corridors and hallways that are often the target of efficiency experts seeking to optimise the net-to-gross floor area ratio and squeeze the most programme space out of limited budgets. Yet it is often these 'unassigned spaces' that are the places we meet and greet and socialise in, providing opportunities for the limited 'street life' that can be enjoyed by those with reduced mobility. From strategically stretching and widening these spaces, providing daylight and views with well-placed windows, places to sit and chat, and doorways with small shelves or ingenious chalkboards (in the case of Ronald McDonald House), the occupants have opportunities to personalise their 'stoops' and initiate communication or simply make their presence known.

There is great art and resourcefulness in getting more out of less, struggling with limited budgets on these projects. It requires working with simple materials and getting elements to do double duty. This is where the inventive powers of the architect are tested to do more than 'stylise' a known quantity, but to combine things in new and unexpected ways. A prime example is the spare but welcoming light and bright shared open kitchen and dining facility in Ronald McDonald House, where residents under great stress are invited (but not obliged) to share the activity of breaking bread in a wonderful setting that may help to momentarily ease the strain.

The search for welcoming forms and hospitable detail is evident throughout the range of projects of this firm. Notable examples include the Humber River Bicycle and Pedestrian Bridge whose wonderful landmark arch provides a delightful place of pause and repose for walkers, runners and cyclists at the mouth of the river, and the handsome new visitor pavilion at the entrance to the Toronto Botanical Garden.

In all these respects, Montgomery Sisam Architects are heirs to a valuable strain of modest humanism in architecture which has too often gotten submerged, not getting the acknowledgment it deserves. By skillfully overcoming the barriers and obstacles to full participation with full and productive lives at all stages and in all conditions, their work is making an important contribution to the creation of an inclusive urban environment that can generously accommodate an increasingly diverse society.

TOP Communal kitchen and dining at Ronald McDonald House Toronto.

BOTTOM Bedroom corridor with a view of north court at Ronald McDonald House Toronto.

poetics of place
nick drake

Poetry is now a marginal art—the volumes are slim in every sense, and anyway poetry has never seen eye to eye with Mammon—yet people still come to it for its gifts; memorial, surprise, consolation, an accommodation or exploration of conflicted emotion and thought, even for moral education, and to look into the confronting mirror of our own strange (and currently endangered) nature. The beauty of much of it is, you can carry it in your head—or in whichever part of yourself you wish to locate it. And although it is 'just words' it can accommodate everything.

Montgomery Sisam's architecture shares many of the same qualities. The projects are almost all not-for-profit, or public buildings. There are no homogenous, generic boxes; each building responds generously and individually to the needs and natures of people and place, reconciling formal constraints and the complex demands of occupants, sites and situations into something surprising, generous, beautiful and memorable. In their exceptional quality and calm dignity, each building enhances the experience of being alive.

They achieve all of that by the transposing power of the imagination. Take the Humber River Bicycle and Pedestrian Bridge. It has become its own destination; it's a structure that answers a necessity, but it also contributes back to the lived experience of the city. People walk to it, walk over it, wander back gazing up at the great white arches of the white steel, or out to the lake framed by the angled cables like harp strings for the wind. It is a bridge as sculpture, invoking the spirits of the Thunderbird and the Serpent, as well as something of the ancient nature of this old crossing place, and it is a magical walk above the water. Cyclists weave a path between the walkers in good-natured, haphazard grace. Passers-by acknowledge each other in the special nature of the space, perhaps because it frames the small dramas of casual, accidental encounters that, in the city, otherwise go unremarked, unrealised. It slows us down enough to notice where we are, and what's happening.

The chapel at the Sisterhood of St John the Divine has a roof shaped like a large, gentle, generous hand. From inside, the only view is sky and scudding clouds, framed by the clerestory window and under-lit by vertical strips of brilliant stained glass. It's a window in which to relish snow falling (as James Joyce wrote, "on the living and the dead"), or to hear the sound of quiet rain. The 'hand' is crafted of handsome slats of warm wood, in sections pleated to the curve of the palm—cupping the held silence, it seemed; or maybe listening to the light and dark outside.

A bridge, a chapel; both built for encounters with the invisible.

At St John's Rehab Hospital, light connects everything. The rehab pool has the proportions and magic of a small temple, a pool of healing. Gently inclined walkways lead down into clear blue water. A huge, tall window shares the light with the calm, echoey surface of the pool.

The original meaning of hospital is "a place of hospitality" whether for visitors, travellers or strangers. The Ronald McDonald House is a calm, cloistered, low-walled refuge in the middle of the city. But this is no austere monastic retreat, no Skellig Michael; the long kitchen area of elegant cooking islands encourages companionableness. There are quiet wooden window seats, like modern versions of settles, on the wide staircases; the red brick of the facade is warm, gentle and familiar; the subtle, optimistic colour-theme of each floor enhances and unifies the whole.

Looking at the body of work accomplished by the practice—hospitals, missions, treatment centres, schools, convents, retirement communities, bridges—these are buildings which compose and integrate the most important aspects and elements of the outside, natural world—light, shade, space, quiet, stillness, harmony—and in doing so, reconnect us to interior experiences of those things, no matter how disordered and chaotic we might feel.

We are all vulnerable to misfortune; whether we are confronting suffering, anxiety, addiction and the fears that underlie those dark times, or whether we need to sit still, to pray, to recover, to watch TV or cook, to sleep peacefully, to get through difficult times, or to be private at times of distress, these are buildings that offer dignity to the occupants; they accommodate the transient dramas of human life. They have generosity, and poetry.

RIGHT Sister Margaret Smith Addictions Treatment Centre.

selected projects

Maple Manor
Tillsonburg, ON
1977

Japan Architect Competition
1978

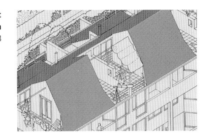

National Housing Design Competition
1979

Beaches Library Addition and Renovation
Toronto, ON
1980

Facelle Company Ltd Head Offices
Toronto, ON
1981

Richview Library
Toronto, ON
1983

University College Union, University of Toronto
Toronto, ON
1986

Forest Hill House Renovation
Toronto, ON
1986

Gilmore Lodge
Fort Erie, ON
1988
joint venture with Chapman Murray

Summer House
Queens County, PEI
1988

Belmont House
Toronto, ON
1988

35 Britain Street
Toronto, ON
1989

Lewson House
Etobicoke, ON
1989

John St Bridge
Toronto, ON
1989
with Wyllie & Ufnal
Ltd Consulting
Engineers

**AR Goudie Eventide
Home**
Kitchener, ON
1993

**Harry W Arthurs
Commons, York
University**
Toronto, ON
1993
joint venture with
Janet Rosenberg and
Studio

**CIBC Yonge and St
Clair Branch
Interior Renovation**
Toronto, ON
1994

Glen Stor Dun Lodge
Cornwall, ON
1994

Bathurst Clark Library
Vaughan, ON
1994

Griffin House
Balsam Lake, ON
1995

Riverside Library
Windsor, ON
1995

**The Humber
River Bicycle and
Pedestrian Bridge**
Toronto, ON
1996
with Delcan
Corporation bridge
engineers

**St Laurent Paperboard
Office Renovation and
Addition**
Toronto, ON
1996

Rapelje Lodge
Welland, ON
1997
joint venture with
Chapman Murray

**Bridge to the Island
Airport**
Toronto, ON
1997
with Dillon Consulting
Ltd Consulting
Engineers

**Dead Centre Study
for the University
of Toronto at
Scarborough**
Scarborough, ON
1998

**CIBC Port Hope
Branch**
Port Hope, ON
1998

Gibbon's Park Bridge
London, ON
1999

**Cardinal Ambrozic
Houses of Providence**
Toronto, ON
2000
joint venture with
Kuwabara Payne
McKenna Blumberg
Architects

Macassa Lodge
Hamilton, ON
2000
joint venture with
Moffat Kinoshita
Architects Inc.

Peter D Clark Home
Nepean, ON
2001
in association with
Bryden Martel

**Trinity Village Care
Centre**
Kitchener, ON
2002

Extendicare Hamilton
Hamilton, ON
2002

**Ottawa Grace
Long Term Care**
Ottawa, ON
2002
joint venture with
Barry J Hobin Architects

Residence in King City
Caledon, ON
2002

**Bird Studies Canada
Headquarters**
Port Rowan, ON
2002

**Isabel and Arthur
Meighen Manor**
Toronto, ON
2003

GE MRI Projects
Across Canada
2003

**Joan Foley Hall,
University of Toronto
at Scarborough**
Scarborough, ON
2003
joint venture with
Baird Sampson Neuert
Architects

Malton Village
Brampton, ON
2003

**Greenwood College
School**
Toronto, ON
2003

**Extendicare Toronto
Rehab Institute**
Toronto, ON
2004

**Holy Cross Catholic
School**
Toronto, ON
2004

**Northland Pointe
Long Term Care**
Port Colborne, ON
2004
joint venture with
Chapman Murray

**Eastern Gap Bridge
Study**
Toronto, ON
2004

**Extendicare Port
Hope**
Port Hope, ON
2004

**The Convent for the
Sisterhood of
St John the Divine**
Toronto, ON
2005

**The George and
Kathy Dembroski
Centre for
Horticulture at the
Toronto Botanical
Garden**
Toronto, ON
2005

**Norview Lodge Long
Term Care Facility**
Simcoe, ON
2005

**Arts and
Administration
Building University
of Toronto at
Scarborough**
Scarborough, ON
2005

Fountainblue Library
Windsor, ON
2005

**Unionville Home
Society**
Markham, ON
2005

Huron Lodge
Windsor, ON
2005

**McMaster Gateway
Competition**
Hamilton, ON
2005

**Regent Park Housing
Competition**
Toronto, ON
2005
joint venture with
Kearns Mancini
Architects

**ROAG House
Competition**
Toronto, ON
2005

**Bob Rumball Home
for the Deaf**
Barrie, ON
2006

**Summer House
Prince Edward Island**
Queens County, PEI
2006

Island Yacht Club
Toronto, ON
2006

**Holland Bloorview
Kids Rehabilitation
Hospital**
Toronto, ON
2006
joint venture with
Stantec Architecture

Lakeview Manor
Beaverton, ON
2006

**Southlands—
Bermuda**
Hamilton, Bermuda
2006
joint venture with
Vogel Architects

Bethany Lodge
Unionville, ON
2007

**First Nations
Technical Institute
Master Plan**
Tyendinaga Mohawk
Territory, ON
2007

**Restoration Services
Centre**
Vaughan, ON
2007

**University of Toronto
St George Campus
Central Examination
Facility**
Toronto, ON
2008

**Centre for Addiction
and Mental Health**
Toronto, ON
2008
joint venture with
Kuwabara Payne
McKenna Blumberg
Architects, Kearns
Mancini Architects

**Sister Margaret
Smith Addiction
Treatment Centre**
Thunder Bay, ON
2009
joint venture with
Form Architecture

**West Park Healthcare
Centre Master Plan**
Toronto, ON
2009

Bruce's Mill
Sustainability
Learning Centre
Study
Stouffville, ON
2009

St Lawrence Market
North Building
Competition
Toronto, ON
2009
joint venture with
Taylor Hazell
Architects

Mount Sinai Centre
for Fertility and
Reproductive Health
Toronto, ON
2009

Greenway
Retirement
Community
Brampton, ON
2009

The Printing Factory
Lofts
Toronto, ON
2009
joint venture with
Chandler Graham

Alderwood Rest
Home
Baddeck, NS
2010
joint venture with
WHW Architects

The York School
Toronto, ON
2010

Fort York Pedestrian
and Cycle Bridge
Toronto, ON
2010

Credit Valley
Conservation
Authority Head
Office Addition
Mississauga, ON
2010

Amica Windsor
Windsor, ON
2010

Tideview Terrace
Digby, NS
2010
joint venture with
WHW Architects

The John C and
Sally Horsfall Eaton
Ambulatory Care
Centre, St John's
Rehab Hospital
Toronto, ON
2010
joint venture with
Farrow Partnership

Ronald McDonald
House Toronto
Toronto, ON
2011

Don Mount Court/
Rivertowne
Toronto, ON
2011
joint venture with
Kearns Mancini

Toronto 2015 Pan/
Para Pan Am Games
Athletes Village
Toronto, ON
2012
joint venture
with HOK, DTAH,
Quadrangle Architects
and Populous
PDC Architects

Tommy Thompson
Park Infrastructure
Project
Toronto, ON
2012

Southdown Institute
East Gwillimbury, ON
2013

Centre for Addiction
and Mental Health
Toronto, ON
2012
joint venture with
Kuwabara Payne
McKenna Blumberg
Architects, Kearns Mancini
Architects and Cannon
Design, PDC Architects

Meadowvale
Sheppard Public
School
Toronto, ON
2013

Kipling Acres
Toronto, ON
2013

Centre of Excellence
for Integrated
Senior's Services
Thunder Bay, ON
2013
joint venture with
Form Architecture

365 Queen Street
West Redevelopment
Toronto, ON
2013

The Granite Club
Toronto, ON
2014

Humber College
Learning Resource
Commons
Toronto, ON
2014
joint venture with
Perkins + Will
PDC Architects

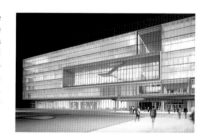

feature project credits

The John C and Sally Horsfall Eaton Ambulatory Care Centre, St John's Rehab Hospital
Location: Toronto, ON
Completion Date: 2010
Client: St John's Rehab Hospital
Partners: Joint venture with Farrow Partnership Architects
Sub-Consultants: Structural—Halcrow Yolles, Mechanical and Electrical—MMM Group, Landscape Architect—Vertechs Design Inc., Civil—EMC Group Ltd, Cost Consultant—Marshall & Murray Inc., Code—Leber Rubes, Acoustics—Aercoustics Engineering Ltd, Lighting—MMM Group
Contractor: Enabling Works—Percon Construction Inc., Main project—Buttcon Ltd
Photographs: Tom Arban

Ronald McDonald House Toronto
Location: Toronto, ON
Completion Date: 2011
Client: Ronald McDonald House Toronto
Sub-Consultants: Structural—Blackwell Bowick Partnership Ltd, Mechanical and Electrical—Crossey Engineering Ltd, Landscape Architect—PMA Landscape Architects Inc., Civil—Crossey Engineering Ltd, Sustainability—Dr Ted Kesik, LEED® Commissioning—CDML, Cost Consultant—AW Hooker Associates, Code—Arencon Inc., Traffic—BA Group, Food Services—Van Velzen and Radchenko Design Associates, Acoustics—Swallow Acoustic Consultants Ltd, Interior Design—Carlyle Design Associates, Energy Modeling—Enersys Analytics Inc., Lighting—Crossey Engineering Ltd
Contractor: Deltera Construction Inc.—a division of Tridel
Photographs: Tom Arban, Donna Griffith, Shai Gil, Michael Graydon

The Bob Rumball Home for the Deaf
Location: Barrie, ON
Completion Date: 2006
Client: Bob Rumball Association for the Deaf
Sub-Consultants: Structural—Blackwell Bowick Partnership Ltd, Mechanical and Electrical—SNC Lavalin Inc., Landscape Architect—Vertechs Design Inc., Civil—Jones Consulting Group Lt., Sustainability Consultant—Enermodal Engineering, Cost Consultant—Turner Townsend cm2r, Code Consultant—Larden Muniak Consulting Inc., Food Services—Van Velzen and Radchenko Design Associates, Signage—Wm Whiteley Ltd
Contractor: Canning Contracting Inc.
Photographs: Tom Arban

Convent for the Sisterhood of St John the Divine
Location: Toronto, ON
Completion Date: 2005
Client: Sisterhood of St John the Divine
Sub-Consultants: Structural—Blackwell Bowick Partnership Ltd, Mechanical—Smith and Andersen Consulting Engineering, Electrical—HH Angus and Associates Ltd, Landscape Architect—Janet Rosenberg and Studio, Civil—EMC Group Ltd, Food Services—Van Velzen and Radchenko Design Associates
Contractor: Dalton Engineering and Construction Ltd
Photographs: Tom Arban

Restoration Services Centre
Location: Vaughan, ON
Completion Date: 2007
Client: Toronto and Region Conservation Authority
Sub-Consultants: Structural—Read Jones Christoffersen Consulting Engineers, Mechanical and Electrical—Enermodal Engineering, Landscape—Toronto and Region Conservation Authority/Ron Koudys Landscape Architect, Civil—EMC Group Ltd, LEED® Consultant—Enermodal Engineering, Cost Consultant—Turner Townsend cm2r
Contractor: Percon Construction Inc.
Photographs: Tom Arban

Summer House Prince Edward Island
Location: Malpeque, Prince Edward Island
Completion Date: 2006
Client: David and Elizabeth Sisam
Sub-Consultants: Structural—Read Jones Christoffersen
Contractor: Carpenters Inc.
Photographs: Yvonne Duivenvoorden, Chatelaine Magazine/Roberto Caruso

Island Yacht Club
Location: Toronto, ON
Completion Date: 2006
Client: Island Yacht Club
Sub-Consultants: Structural—Halsall Associates Ltd,
Mechanical and Electrical—SNC Lavalin Inc., Landscape— Janet
Rosenberg and Studio, Cost Consultant—Turner Townsend cm2r,
Code Consultant—Larden Muniak Consulting Inc., Food Services—
Van Velzen and Radchenko Design Associates, Signage—Wm
Whiteley Ltd
Contractor: Metron Construction Inc.
Photographs: Tom Arban

Greenwood College School
Location: Toronto, ON
Completion Date: 2003
Client: Greenwood College School
Sub-Consultants: Structural—Read Jones Christoffersen Consulting
Engineers, Mechanical—Keen Engineering Company Ltd, Electrical—
Carinci Burt Rogers Engineering Inc., Civil—Sernas Group, Cost—JS
Watson and Associates Ltd, Food Services—Van Velzen and
Radchenko Design Associates, Acoustics—Aercoustics Engineering
Ltd, Planning—RE Millward
Contractor: JS Watson and Associates Ltd
Photographs: Tom Arban

Extendicare Port Hope
Location: Port Hope, ON
Completion Date: 2004
Client: Extendicare Canada
Sub-Consultants: Structural—Read Jones Christoffersen Consulting
Engineers, Mechanical and Electrical—Crossey Engineering Ltd,
Landscape—Vertechs Design, Civil—Wills Associates, Cost—Turner
Townsend cm2r, Code—Larden Muniak Consulting Inc., Food
Service—AJ Watts Consulting, Interior Design—Newcombe Design
Contractor: Maple Reinders Constructors Ltd
Photographs: Steven Evans

Extendicare Rouge Valley
Location: Toronto, ON
Completion Date: 2003
Client: Extendicare Canada
Sub-Consultants: Structural—Read Jones Christoffersen Consulting
Engineers, Mechanical and Electrical—Crossey Engineering Ltd,
Landscape—Vertechs Design, Civil—EMC Group, Cost—Turner
Townsend cm2r, Code—Larden Muniak Consulting Inc., Food
Service—AJ Watts Consulting, Interior Design—Newcombe Design
Contractor: Buttcon Ltd
Photographs: Steven Evans

**University of Toronto St George Campus Central Examination
Facility**
Location: Toronto, ON
Completion Date: 2008
Client: University of Toronto
Sub-Consultants: Structural—Read Jones Christoffersen,
Mechanical and Electrical—Crossey Engineering Ltd, Sustainability/
LEED®—Enermodal Engineering, Code—Leber Rubes Inc.,
Commissioning—VSC Group Inc., Acoustics—Swallow Acoustic
Consultants Ltd, Elevator—Ayling Consulting Services Inc.,
Signage—Wm Whiteley Ltd, Lighting—Crossey Engineering Ltd
Contractor: Eastern Construction
Photographs: Tom Arban, Shai Gil

Holland Bloorview Kids Rehabilitation Hospital
Location: Toronto, ON
Completion Date: 2006
Client: Holland Bloorview Kids Rehabilitation Hospital
Partners: Joint venture with Stantec Architecture
Sub-Consultants: Structural—Halcrow Yolles, Mechanical and
Electrical—HH Angus and Associates Ltd, Landscape—Vertechs
Design Inc., Cost—Turner Townsend cm2r, Code—Larden Muniak
Consulting Inc., Commissioning—CFMS Consulting Inc., Food
Services—Marrack and Associates, Acoustics—Valcoustics Canada
Ltd, Elevator—KJA Consulting, Interiors—Carlyle Design Associates
Contractor: Ellis Don Corporation
Photographs: Tom Arban, Paul Kozlowski, Richard Johnston

**The George and Kathy Dembroski Centre for Horticulture
at the Toronto Botanical Garden**
Location: Toronto, ON
Completion Date: 2005
Client: Toronto Botanical Garden
Sub-Consultants: Structural—Blackwell Bowick Partnership Ltd,
Mechanical and Electrical—MMM Group Landscape—Lead
Designers—PMA Landscape Architects with Thomas Sparling Inc.,
Landscape—Entry Garden—Martin Wade Landscape Architects with
Piet Oudolf, Landscape—Planting Design—Paul Ehnes, Landscape—
Horticulturalist, Sustainability—Enermodal Engineering
Contractor: Dalton Engineering and Construction Ltd
Photographs: Tom Arban

Norview Lodge Long Term Care Facility
Location: Simcoe, ON
Completion Date: 2005
Client: Regional Municipality of Haldimand—Norfolk County
Sub-Consultants: Structural—Halcrow Yolles, Mechanical and
Electrical—MMM Group Landscape—Ron Koudys Landscape
Architect Inc., Civil—G Douglas Vallee Ltd, Cost—Turner Townsend
cm2r, Food Services—AJ Watts Consulting
Contractor: The Atlas Corporation
Photographs: Tom Arban

Bird Studies Canada Headquarters
Location: Port Rowan, ON
Completion Date: 2002
Client: Bird Studies Canada
Partners: Contract Administration done by Eric Connolly Architects
Sub-Consultants: Structural—Blackwell Bowick Partnership Ltd,
Mechanical—Tou and Associates, Electrical—McDonnell Engineering
Inc., Civil—MC Engineering, Cost—Turner Townsend cm2r
Contractor: Ivan Francis Construction
Photographs: Steven Evans

The Cardinal Ambrozic Houses of Providence
Location: Toronto, ON
Completion Date: 2000
Client: Providence Healthcare
Partners: Joint venture with Kuwabara Payne McKenna Blumberg
Sub-Consultants: Structural—Read Jones Christoffersen Consulting Engineers, Mechanical and Electrical—Crossey Engineering Ltd, Landscape—Vertechs Design Inc., Cost—Helyar and Associates, Food Services—Marrack Watt Inc., Interiors—Newcombe and Associates
Contractor: Bondfield Construction
Photographs: Steven Evans

Centre for Addiction and Mental Health Transitional Client Care Building
Location: Toronto, ON
Completion Date: 2008
Client: Centre for Addiction and Mental Health
Partners: Joint venture consortium C3 (Kuwabara Payne McKenna Blumberg Architects, Montgomery Sisam Architects, Kearns Mancini Architects Inc.)
Sub-Consultants: Structural—Read Jones Christoffersen Consulting Engineers, Mechanical—MMM Group, Electrical—Crossey Engineering Ltd, Landscape—Janet Rosenberg and Studio, Civil—MMM Group, Cost—Marshall and Murray, Interiors—C3, Urban Design—Urban Strategies Inc.
Contractor: Eastern Construction
Photographs: Tom Arban

Centre for Addiction and Mental Health—Intergenerational Wellness Centre, Bell Gateway Building and Parking and Utilities Building
Location: Toronto, ON
Completion Date: 2012
Client: Centre for Addiction and Mental Health
Partners: Joint venture consortium C3 (Kuwabara Payne McKenna Blumberg Architects, Montgomery Sisam Architects and Kearns Mancini Architects) were responsible for the design exemplar. C3 + Cannon Design were the Planning, Design and Compliance Architects, responsible for the Project Specific Output Specifications. Stantec Architects were the architects for the Design, Build, Finance and Maintain consortium responsible for the design through construction. They are the Architects of Record
Sub-Consultants: Structural—Read Jones Christoffersen Consulting Engineers, Mechanical—MMM Group, Electrical—Crossey Engineering Ltd, Landscape—Janet Rosenberg and Studio, Civil—MMM Group, Cost—Marshall and Murray, Food Services— Kaizen, Interiors—C3, Urban Design—Urban Strategies Inc.
Contractor: Carillion Canada
Photographs: Tom Arban

Don Mount Court/Rivertowne
Location: Toronto, ON
Completion Date: 2010
Client: Intracorp—Marion Hill for the Toronto Community Housing Corporation
Partners: Joint venture with Kearns Mancini Architects
Sub-Consultants: Structural—Kazmar & Associates Ltd, Mechanical and Electrical—MV Shore Associates Ltd, Landscape—MBTW Group, Civil—MMM Group, Cost—Altus Heylar Cost Consulting Code—Randall Brown and Associates, Acoustics— Swallow Acoustics
Contractor: Intracorp/Marion Hill Development Corp.
Photographs: Tom Arban

Printing Factory Lofts
Location: Toronto, ON
Completion Date: 2010
Client: Beaverbrook Homes
Partners: Joint venture with Chandler Graham Architects
Sub-Consultants: Structural—Blackwell Bowick Partnership Ltd, Mechanical and Electrical—Novatrend Engineering Group Ltd, Cost—Helyar Construction Cost Management, Code—Randall Brown and Associates Ltd
Contractor: Beaverbrook Homes
Photographs: Tom Arban

The Humber River Bicycle and Pedestrian Bridge
Location: Toronto, ON
Completion Date: 1996
Client: City of Toronto
Partners: In collaboration with Delcan Corporation
Sub-Consultants: Engineers—Delcan Corporation, Landscape— Ferris and Quinn Associates Inc., Public Artwork—Environmental Artworks Studio
Contractor: Dominion Bridge
Photographs: Tom Arban, Bob Burley

The Arts and Administration Building at the University of Toronto at Scarborough
Location: Scarborough, ON
Completion Date: 2005
Client: University of Toronto
Sub-Consultants: Structural—Halcrow Yolles, Mechanical—MMM Group, Electrical—Carinci Burt Rogers Engineering Inc., Landscape— Janet Rosenberg and Studio, Sustainability—Enermodal Engineering, Code—Leber Rubes Inc., Acoustics—Aercoustics Engineering Ltd
Contractor: Kenaidan Contracting Ltd
Photographs: Tom Arban

Tommy Thompson Park Infrastructure Project
Location: Toronto, ON
Completion Date: 2012
Client: Toronto and Region Conservation Authority
Sub-Consultants: Structural—Halsall Engineering, Mechanical and Electrical—MV Shore Associates Ltd, Cost—Turner Townsend cm2r
Contractor: Martinway Contracting Ltd
Photographs: Ben Rahn, Jinny Kim

additional photo credits

introduction

Humber River Bicycle and Pedestrian Bridge—Tom Arban

architecture as citizen

Facelle Company Ltd—Bob Burley

Bathurst Clark Library—Bob Burley

Bird Studies Headquarters—Steven Evans

Greenwood College School—Steven Evans

Ronald McDonald House Toronto—Tom Arban

Centre for Addiction and Mental Health watercolour—Quang Ho

light and air

Royal Chelsea Hospital—Peter Aprahamian

Cambridge, UK—unknown

Zonestraal Sanitorium—Michel Kievits

economy of means, generosity of ends

St Petersburg—Matt Galvin

Luis Barragan House—Jose Alvarez Checa

Centre for Integrated Seniors Services rendering—Norm Li

Peter D Clarke Centre—David Whittaker

Greenwood College School—Steven Evans

Sister Margaret Smith Addictions Treatment Centre—Tom Arban

transcending expectations

Holland Bloorview Kids Rehabilitation Hospital—Tom Arban

Cardinal Ambrozic Houses of Providence—Steven Evans

Isabel and Arthur Meighen Manor—Steven Evans

Arts and Administration Building, University of Toronto at Scarborough—Tom Arban

the space between

University of Virginia—David Sisam

Saynatsalo Town Hall—Marjut Dunker

Charleston House—David Sisam

Kings Road House—© J Paul Getty Trust. Used with permission.

Julius Shulman Photography Archive, Research Library at the Getty Research Institute (2004.R.10)

an architecture of generous inclusion

Ronald McDonald House Toronto—Tom Arban

poetics of place

Sister Margaret Smith Addictions Treatment Centre—Tom Arban

Montgomery Sisam Architects in joint venture with Form Architecture

selected awards

2011 Toronto Urban Design Awards
Award of Excellence—Visions and Master Plans
The Fort York Pedestrian and Cycle Bridge
Toronto, ON

2011 Toronto Urban Design Awards
Honourable Mention—Private Buildings in
Context-Mid-Rise
The Printing Factory Lofts
Toronto, ON

**2011 International Academy for Health
and Design**
Highly Commended—International Mental
Health Design
7th Design & Health World Congress and
Exhibition, Boston
Sister Margaret Smith Addictions Treatment
Centre
Thunder, Bay ON

**2011 Paul Oberman Award for Outstanding
Achievement in the Field of Architecture and
Design—Pug Awards, The 7th Annual People's
Choice Awards for Architecture**
The Printing Factory Lofts
Toronto, ON

2011 Royal Architectural Institute of Canada
Architectural Firm of the Year Award

**2010 June Callwood Outstanding
Achievement Award**
for Voluntarism in Ontario

2009 Toronto Construction Association
"Best of the Best" Award for Green
Building Culture

2009 Toronto Urban Design Award
Honourable Mention—Holland Bloorview Kids
Rehabilitation Hospital
Toronto, ON

**2009 International Academy for Health
and Design**
Healthcare Design Project Academy Award
6th Design & Health World Congress and
Exhibition, Singapore
Centre for Addiction and Mental Health, Phase 1A
Toronto, ON

**2009 Ontario Association of Architects Award
of Excellence**
Island Yacht Club
Toronto, ON

**2008 Ontario WoodWORKS
Multi-Unit Wood Design Award**
Bob Rumball Home for the Deaf
Barrie, ON

**2008 Sustainable Architecture and Building
Award—SAB Magazine**
Restoration Services Centre, Toronto and Region
Conservation Authority
Vaughan, ON

**2008 Ontario Association of Architects Award
of Excellence**
Holland Bloorview Kids Rehabilitation Hospital
Toronto, ON

**2008 Ontario Association of Architects Award
of Excellence**
George and Kathy Dembroski Centre for
Horticulture, Toronto Botanical Garden
Toronto, ON

2007 NAIOP Real Estate Excellence Awards
Finalist, Green Award of the Year
Restoration Services Centre, Toronto and Region
Conservation Authority
Vaughan, ON

2007 Ontario WoodWORKS
Wood Advocate Award—Architect

2007 Ontario WoodWORKS
Green Design Award
Restoration Services Centre, Toronto and Region
Conservation Authority
Vaughan, ON

**2007 Outside the Box Awards—*Building
Magazine***
Architecturally Innovative Design
Holland Bloorview Kids Rehabilitation Hospital
Toronto Botanical Garden
Toronto, ON

**2007 International Academy for Health and
Design**
Healthcare Design Project Academy Award
5th Design & Health World Congress and
Exhibition, Glasgow
Holland Bloorview Kids Rehabilitation Hospital
Toronto, ON

**2007 Greater Toronto Home Builders
Association Home Builders Awards**
Project of the Year—Low-Rise
Don Mount Court/Rivertowne
Toronto, ON

**2006 Lieutenant Governor's Design Award—
Nova Scotia**
Richmond Villa Long Term Care Replacement
Facility
Halifax, Nova Scotia

2006 Design Exchange Award
Honourable Mention
Arts and Administration Building, University of
Toronto at Scarborough
Toronto, ON

**2006 Outside the Box Award—*Building
Magazine***
User Friendly Urban Design
Arts and Administration Building,
University of Toronto at Scarborough
Toronto, ON

2006 City of Toronto—Green Toronto Award
Green Design
Toronto Botanical Garden
Toronto, ON

2006 City of Toronto Environmental Award
Award of Excellence
Toronto Botanical Garden
Toronto, ON

2005 Ottawa Urban Design Awards
Award of Excellence, Urban Infill
Ottawa Grace Long Term Care
Ottawa, ON

2005 Impact on Learning Award
(The Council of Education Facility Planners
International)
Non-traditional Learning Spaces
Greenwood College School
Toronto, ON

**2005 Toronto Architecture & Urban
Design Awards**
Honourable Mention: Master Plans
Centre for Addiction and Mental Health
Master Plan
Toronto, ON

2004 Canada's Top 100 Employers
Mediacorp's Top 100 Employers designation
published in *Maclean's magazine*

2003 Canada's Top 100 Employers
Mediacorp's Top 100 Employers
designation published in *Maclean's magazine*

2003 WOOD WORKS Award
Jury's Choice Award
Wood Design Institutional Category
Bird Studies Canada Headquarters
Port Rowan, ON

2003 Wood Design Award
Award of Merit
Bird Studies Canada Headquarters
Port Rowan, ON

2001 National Post/Design Exchange Award
Gold Award
Cardinal Ambrozic Houses of Providence
Scarborough, ON

2001 Canadian Architect Award
Award of Merit
Bird Studies Canada Headquarters
Port Rowan, ON

2000 Canadian Architect Award
Award of Excellence
Trinity Village Care Centre
Kitchener, ON

2000 Top Six Co-op Employers on the Planet
Dalhousie University's Co-operative Program

2000 City of Toronto Urban Design Award
Element or Building Award
Cardinal Ambrozic Houses of Providence
Toronto, ON

**2000 Ontario Association of Architects Award
of Excellence**
Honourable Mention
CIBC Branch
Port Hope, ON

1998 Canadian Architect Award
Award of Excellence
Dead Centre: Additions and alterations to the
University of Toronto at Scarborough
Scarborough, ON

1997 Canadian Architect Award
Award of Merit
Cardinal Ambrozic Houses of Providence
Scarborough, ON

**1997 International Waterfront Centre
Annual Award**
Excellence on the Waterfront
Humber River Bicycle and Pedestrian Bridge
Toronto, ON

1997 Apple Canada/Financial Post Award
Design Effectiveness Award
Humber River Bicycle and Pedestrian Bridge
Toronto, ON

1997 City of Toronto Urban Design Award
Humber River Bicycle and Pedestrian Bridge
Toronto, ON

**1997 Michael V and Wanda Plachta
Architectural Award**
Humber River Bicycle and Pedestrian Bridge
Toronto, ON

**1997 Ontario Association of Architects Award
of Excellence**
Humber River Bicycle and Pedestrian Bridge
Toronto, ON

1996 Governor General's Award
Humber River Bicycle and Pedestrian Bridge
Toronto, ON

1996 Canadian Institute of Steel Construction
Ontario Steel Design Award
Humber River Bicycle and Pedestrian Bridge
Toronto, ON

1995 City of Etobicoke Urban Design Award
Award of Excellence
Humber River Bicycle and Pedestrian Bridge
Toronto, ON

1995 City of North York Urban Design Award
Award of Excellence
Harry W Arthurs Common, York University
North York, ON

1994 Canadian Architect Award
Award of Excellence
Humber River Bicycle and Pedestrian Bridge
Toronto/Etobicoke, ON

1993 City of Toronto Urban Design Award
Honourable Mention
John Street Pedestrian Bridge
Toronto, ON

**1992 Ontario Association of Architects/
Canadian House and Home Magazine
Residential Design Award**
Honourable Mention
Renovation to 59 Dunloe Road
Toronto, ON

1991 Canadian Architect Award
Award of Excellence
Bathurst Clark Resource Library
Vaughan, ON

**1991 Ontario Association of Architects Award
of Excellence**
John Street Pedestrian Bridge
Toronto, ON

**1990 Competition for the Technical University
of Nova Scotia School of Architecture Addition**
Honourable Mention
Halifax, Nova Scotia

1987 Canadian Architect Yearbook Award
Award of Excellence
John Street Pedestrian Bridge
Toronto, ON

1986 Ontario Renews Award
Honourable Mention
Richview Library
Etobicoke ON

1985 Canadian Architect Yearbook Award
Award of Excellence
Country House
Orangeville, ON

1984 Ontario Renews Awards
Honourable Mention
Beaches Library
Toronto, ON

1982 Energy Efficient Housing Competition
First Place
Ministry of Energy, Government of Ontario
Hamilton, ON

**1980 National Competition for the Design of
Edmonton City Hall**
Merit Award
Edmonton AB
*with Byfield Langford Architects Ltd, Edmonton

1979 National Housing Design Competition
Mention
Ontario Region

1979 National Housing Design Competition
Special Mention
Quebec Region

1979 National Housing Design Competition
Second Prize
Atlantic Region

**1978 Shinkenchiku Residential Design
Competition**
First Prize
Japan Architect magazine: open, world-wide design
competition

biographies

CONTRIBUTORS

Nick Drake

Nick Drake is a British poet, novelist and screenwriter. His first poetry collection, *The Man in the White Suit*, 1999, won the Waterstone's/ Forward Prize for Best First Collection. It was also a Poetry Book Society Recommendation. His second collection, *From the Word Go* appeared in 2007. Following an invitation from Cape Farewell to sail around Svalbard in the Arctic, he collaborated with United Visual Artists on HIGH ARCTIC, an installation for London's National Maritime Museum, 2011. The resulting poems are gathered in *The Farewell Glacier*, 2012. Nick's screenplays include *Romulus, My Father*, starring Eric Bana, which won four awards at the Australian Film Institute Awards, including Best Film. His adaptation of *STASILAND*, based on Anna Funder's award-winning book, was commissioned by the National Theatre. He has written the libretto for a full-length opera for English National Opera, in collaboration with director Deborah Warner and composer Tansy Davies. *Nefertiti: The Book of the Dead*, 2006, was shortlisted for the CWA's Historical Mystery Dagger award. *Tutankhamun: The Book of Shadows*, 2009, was a *Publishers Weekly* Top 100 Books Selection. The final novel in the trilogy, *Egypt: The Book of Chaos* followed in 2011.

Ken Greenberg, FRAIC, AIA Associate

Former Director of Urban Design and Architecture for the City of Toronto, Architect and Urban Designer Ken Greenberg is principal of Greenberg Consultants, which focuses on campus master planning, regional growth management, new community planning and the rejuvenation of downtowns, waterfronts and neighbourhoods. His projects are based internationally in such cities as Toronto, Amsterdam, Paris, Minneapolis, New York, Boston, Montreal, Washington, Detroit and San Juan, Puerto Rico. He applies a holistic approach to city-building, crossing traditional boundaries and working in team settings to collaborate with professionals from a variety of disciplines to restore the vitality, relevance and sustainability of the public realm in urban life. His work has garnered awards from the Canadian Institute of Planners, the City of Toronto, the American Planning Association and several journals on architecture. He has taught design at Harvard's Graduate School of Design, the University of Michigan and other universities in North America and abroad. He was the recipient of the 2010 American Institute of Architects Thomas Jefferson Award for public design excellence and is the author of *Walking Home: The Life and Lessons of a City Builder* published by Random House.

Beth Kapusta, BES BArch

Beth Kapusta is a Toronto-based architecture critic. Her writings on architecture, urbanism, and landscape have appeared in Canadian newspapers including the *Globe and Mail* and *National Post* as well as national and international publications—*Domus*, *Architectural Record*, *Architecture*, and the *Huffington Post*, and Canadian magazines including *Azure*, where she has been a Contributing Editor since 2002. She is co-author of *Yolles: A Canadian Engineering Legacy*. She has taught urban design at the University of Waterloo School of Architecture, where she received her Bachelor of Architecture degree in 1991. Beth has been a collaborator in numerous projects and winning competitions that demonstrate her passion for Toronto's urban and cultural landscape, including June Callwood Park, HTO Park, Sugar Beach, Dundas Square, and buildings such as the University of Toronto Faculty of Law, the Ivey School of Business and the Perimeter Institute. Her translational communication work around sustainability ranges from an advisory role for the television series *The Word's Greenest Homes*, to involvement founding Cape Farewell Canada, an organisation catalysing a cultural response to climate change. She was one of 20 artists and scientists to participate in Cape Farewell's 2010 Arctic expedition.

Bruce Kuwabara, OAA, FRAIC, AIA, RIBA

Bruce Kuwabara is a founding partner of Kuwabara Payne McKenna Blumberg (KPMB) in Toronto and has been recognised as one of Canada's leading architects. He was the recipient of the RAIC Gold Medal in 2006 and was invested as an Officer of the Order of Canada in 2012. He has received public and professional acclaim for several projects of national and international significance, including Canada's National Ballet School, the Gardiner Museum, and The Bell Lightbox for the Toronto International Film Festival, as well as the Canadian Museum of Nature in Ottawa and Manitoba Hydro Place in Winnipeg. Current work includes the Athletes Village for the 2015 Pan American Games, the new Kellogg School of Management at Northwestern University, the Remai Art Gallery of Saskatchewan, the Global Centre for Pluralism for the Aga Khan Foundation and the Departments of Economics and International Initiatives at Princeton University. Bruce has taught at the Faculty of Architecture, Landscape and Design at the University of Toronto and at Harvard's Graduate School of Design. He is the first Chair of Waterfront Toronto's Design Review Panel, and is a member of the Board of Directors for the Canadian Centre for Architecture in Montreal.

PRINCIPALS

Ed Applebaum, BArch, OAA, MRAIC, LEED®AP

Born in Winnipeg in 1956, Ed Applebaum's design training began at the University of Manitoba. After graduation from Environmental Studies, his early career experiences included architectural work in several provinces in Western Canada. After coming to Ontario, he graduated from the School of Architecture at the University of Waterloo in 1984. Following a four-year internship, he joined Montgomery Sisam Architects and became a principal with the firm in 1999. Throughout his career, Ed has been an active member of the local design and construction community. As a member of the board for the Toronto Construction Association since 2007, Ed currently acts as Chair for the Allied Professions Committee. In addition, he serves the local community by chairing several boards for the Kehilla not-for-profit housing corporation, an arm of the United Jewish Federation of Toronto.

Robert Davies, BArch, OAA, MRAIC

Robert Davies was born in Toronto in 1955 and received a Bachelor of Architecture in 1979 from the University of Toronto, at a time that Terry Montgomery and David Sisam were teaching. Robert's early experience included work at the offices of Barton Myers Architect, Stinson Montgomery Sisam Architects, William Grierson Architect and the City of Toronto Urban Design Group under the tutelage of Ken Greenberg. Rejoining the newly formed Montgomery Sisam Architects in 1987, he became a principal in 1999. He is currently a visiting critic of thesis students at the University of Toronto. In addition to his work at the practice he is President of Environmental Defence—an ENGO dedicated to improving the environment and human health, and a Director at Cape Farewell North America—a charitable organisation that initiates a cultural response to climate change.

Santiago Kunzle, Dipl. Arch., LEED® AP

Santiago Kunzle was born in Bariloche, Argentina in 1964 and received a degree in Architecture in 1988 from the University of Cordoba in Argentina. Santiago's early experience included work at several offices including that of renowned Argentinean Architect Miguel Angel Roca where he participated in projects throughout Argentina and Bolivia. After graduating, Santiago worked for Cordoba's Provincial Ministry of Public Works where he integrated multidisciplinary teams that designed many of the province's public buildings including a paediatric hospital. Santiago immigrated to Canada in 1990 where he joined Montgomery Sisam Architects becoming a principal in 2001. Santiago was named delegate to the World Green Building Council in 2008 and currently sits on the City of Vaughan Design Review Panel.

Alice Liang, BArch, OAA, MRAIC

Alice Liang was born in Taiwan in 1954 and immigrated to Toronto, Canada in 1967 with her family. She received her Bachelor of Architecture degree in 1977 from the University of Toronto where David Sisam and Terry Montgomery were both teaching. Alice started her career working in the office of Jack Diamond for seven years after graduation and registered with the OAA in 1981. She subsequently worked in London, England and had her own practice before joining Montgomery Sisam Architects in 2001, becoming principal in 2006. Alice participates regularly as visiting critic at Ryerson and Humber College, as well as mentoring master thesis students from Universities of Toronto, Waterloo and Ryerson. She is an active member of the Advisory Committee for the International Academy for Design and Health, an organisation based in Sweden, with the focus on the global exchange of knowledge to enhance the health and wellbeing of all people.

Daniel Ling, BArch, OAA, MRAIC, AIA, LEED®AP

Daniel Ling was born in Hong Kong in 1976 and immigrated to Toronto, Canada in 1987. He attended Carleton University School of Architecture where he received a Bachelor of Architecture in 1999. Prior to completing his studies, Daniel worked onsite with several construction firms in Hong Kong. Upon graduating, he moved to New York City where he worked for four years, becoming registered as an architect in New York State in 2003. That same year, he moved to Toronto and joined Montgomery Sisam Architects. He became principal in the firm in 2007. Daniel has served as a member of the Infrastructure Advisory Board for the Department of Foreign Affairs and International Trade, an organisation with a focus to promote the Canadian infrastructure industries, their brand, and expertise.

Terry Montgomery, BArch, OAA, FRAIC

Terry Montgomery was born in Toronto in 1944 and received a Bachelor of Architecture from the University of Toronto in 1969. As a student Terry worked in the offices of JD Postma in Amsterdam and Walter Niehaus in Zurich. After graduating he worked briefly for John Andrews, Architect in Toronto as well as Clifford and Lawrie Architects. He was a founding principal of Stinson Montgomery Sisam Architects in 1978 and subsequently Montgomery Sisam Architects in 1987. Terry taught at the University of Toronto, School of Architecture, as Lecturer and then as Assistant Professor, between 1973 and 1983. He has been Adjunct Professor at Dalhousie University and visiting critic at the University of Waterloo and Ryerson University. In 1998 Terry was named a Fellow of the Royal Architectural Institute of Canada and in 2009 he was awarded the Circle of Honour Award by Holland Bloorview Kids Rehabilitation Hospital.

David Sisam, BArch, OAA, FRAIC, LEED®AP

David Sisam was born in Oxford, UK in 1945 and received a Bachelor of Architecture from the University of Toronto in 1969. David worked for several offices in London, UK and Toronto including Chamberlin Powell and Bon, John B Parkin, Clifford and Lawrie and Marani Rounthwaite and Dick. He began his own practice in 1974. He was a founding principal of Stinson Montgomery Sisam Architects in 1978 and of Montgomery Sisam Architects in 1987. A Lecturer and Assistant Professor at the School of Architecture, University of Toronto from 1972 to 1983, David has been a visiting studio instructor at Dalhousie University and a visiting critic at the University of Waterloo and Ryerson University. He currently sits on the City of Toronto Design Review Panel. David was named a Fellow of the Royal Architectural Institute of Canada in 1998 and in 2009 received the Arbor Award for volunteer service to the University of Toronto.

staff lists

CURRENT

Ed Applebaum (Principal)
Evelyn Casquenette
Brad Collard
Robert Davies (Principal)
Rosalie Dawson
Jason Dobbin (Senior Associate)
Sandra Dorenberg (Controller)
Matt Galvin (Associate)
Sarah Gibney
Phil Goodfellow (Associate)
Gordon Green (Senior Associate)
William Harispuru
Marie Hernandez
Vanessa Hii
Kevin Hutchinson
Jin Kim (IT Manager)
Jinny Hye Kim
Santiago Kunzle (Principal)
Alice Liang (Principal)
Daniel Ling (Principal)
Enda McDonagh
Gavin McLachlan
Sarah Miller
Terry Montgomery (Principal)
Michael Nally
Lyn Northey
Leslie Parker (Associate)
Hussain Patwary
Tony Ross (Associate)
Dave Saunders
Tanja Serdar
David Sisam (Principal)
Joel Starkman (Senior Associate)

Elliott Sturtevant
Kirsten Thompson (Associate)
Amy Truong
Melissa Verge (Marketing Director)
Shannon Wiley
Clement Zeng (Associate)

PAST*

Lynn Abernethey
Stuart Adams
David Agro
Kili Akua
Logan Amos
Tricia Arabian
Fatima Arauja
Heather Asquith
Emmanuel Ates
Wayne Austin
Manmeet Bachhas
Charles Barrett
Erika Barrientos
Tomek Bartczak
Yasmeen Bebal
Emily Best
Graham Bolton
Maya Bou Hadir
Sydney Browne
Marcia Bruce
Chris Burbidge
James Burkitt
Calvin Brook
Orla Canavan
John Ciarmela
Ross Carter-
    Wingrove
Nicola Casciato
Anna Cascioli
Terry Cecil
Edward Chan
Cecilia Chen
Sue Jean Chung

Jaegap Chung
Eric Connolly
Martin Corpeno
Gustavo Corredor
Isaac Cravit
Karen Curtis
Catia Da Silva
Leland Dadson
Greg Demaiter
Robert D'Errico
Martin Dolan
Ellen Dowswell
Tan Duong
Amin Ebrahim
Bie Engelen
Julie Finkle
Robbie Frame
Carson Fung
Ivana Gazic
Robbie Glass
Kurt Glauser
Nathan Goodchild
Trevore Grams
Maggie Greyson
Andrew Guiry
Paul Harris
Joanne Heinen
Dustin Hooper
Kai Hotson
Samer Hout
Julian Jaffary
Leslie Jen
Patrick Kennedy

Sylvia Kim
Tom Knezic
Rossen Kolev
Gosia Komorski
Matus Krajnak
Nelson Kwong
Jan Ladisch
Laura Langridge
Stéphane Leblanc
Michael Leckman
David Lee
Minwoo Lee
Jeffrey Leong-Poi
Ho Yin Patrick Li
Alison Licsik
Marty Lillepold
Ella Lin
Kevin Lindores
Evenlyn Lo
Lowell Lo
Michael Lo
Nick Losurdo
Shahid Mahmood
Jennifer Mallard
James Mallinson
Mehdi Marzyari
Jim McDonald
Clare McEvoy
Victoria McGlade
Anne McIlroy
Antonio Medina
Doron Meinhard
Fernando Mejia

Leo Mieles
Ryan Mitchell
Pauline Moebus
Dana Morales
Chris Mosiadz
Jalila Muhammad
Richard Myers
Doug Oliver
David Ospalak
Michael Paquette
Amit Patel
Neda Pavela
Elizabeth Pentek
Marco Polo
Scott Pomeroy
James Rice
Donald Ryan
Judith Sanz-Sole
Lisa Sawatsky
David Siahan
Jalima Simancas
Daniel Simard
Tracy Singleton
Tina Smith
Rob Smyth
Dave Smythe
Sebastiano Spataro
Don Squires
Christopher Stevens
Eryn Stoddart
Dawn Stremler
Kevin Sugden
Anna Sulikowska

Esther Sun
Michael Szabo
Chei-Wei Tai
Leonard Temes
James Tenyenhuis
Marco Travaglini
Angela Tsementzis
Roman Turczyn
Jennifer Turner
Cameron Turvey
Grace Tyono
Siri Ursin
Jeffrey Veffer
Sybil Wa
Rachel Wallace
Mark Warner
Andrzej Wodkiewicz
Phoebe Wong
Keyu Xiong
Coco Xiong
Katarzyna Zapoloch
Javier Zeller
Tao Zeng
Chung Zhang
Joe Zingaro

* Every attempt was
made to compile a
comprehensive list.
A sincere apology
to those who have
been inadvertently
excluded from the list.

acknowledgements

We owe a great deal of gratitude to our clients for both the confidence that they have shown in us and for challenging and supporting us through the complex process of bringing projects to fruition.

We thank our staff both past and present whose dedication, enthusiasm and talent is evident on the pages of this book; and our administrative staff for keeping us organised and solvent.

We are grateful to the broad range of exceptional consultants, contractors and in some cases joint venture partners who have been vital team players in the evolution of these projects.

In the production of this book, a big thank you goes to Melissa Verge who has coordinated the process and nurtured this, our first publishing enterprise, on behalf of our office. A thank you to Kevin Hutchinson and Elliott Sturtevant who prepared the drawings for this publication and to Tom Arban, Steven Evans and the other photographers whose work fills these pages.

We are also grateful to Beth Kapusta for her perceptive historic overview of the practice and to Bruce Kuwabara, Ken Greenberg and Nick Drake who took time out of their extremely busy schedules to interpret our work and generously share their insights. Thanks to Duncan McCorquodale for his patience, support and interest in the work of our office, and to Mónica Oliveira who did the book design.

Finally, a big thank you to friends and family members whose unwavering support through the inevitable ups and downs of practice have allowed us to pursue our goal of making memorable places.

Artifice books on architecture
10A Acton Street
London
WC1X 9NG

t. +44 (0)207 713 5097
f. +44 (0)207 713 8682
sales@artificebooksonline.com
www.artificebooksonline.com

All opinions expressed within this publication are those of the authors and not necessarily of the publisher.

Designed by Mónica Oliveira at Artifice books on architecture.

British Library Cataloguing-in-Publication Data.
A CIP record for this book is available from the British Library.

ISBN 978 1 908967 08 4

Every effort has been made to trace the copyright holders, but if any have been inadvertently overlooked the necessary arrangements will be made at the first opportunity.

Artifice books on architecture is an environmentally responsible company. *Place and Occasion* is printed on sustainably sourced paper.